A CENTENNIAL CELEBRATION OF

THE BRIGHT STAR RESTAURANT

A CENTENNIAL CELEBRATION OF

The Bright Star Restaurant

THE BRIGHT STAR FAMILY

With NIKI SEPSAS

With Tributes by RICHARD SHELBY and GENE STALLINGS

THE UNIVERSITY OF ALABAMA PRESS • TUSCALOOSA

The University of Alabama Press
Tuscaloosa, Alabama 35487-0380
uapress.ua.edu

The recipes in this book are intended to be followed as written by the author. Results will vary.

Hardcover edition published 2007.
Paperback edition published 2018.

Typeface: AGaramond

Cover design: Michele Myatt Quinn

Paperback ISBN: 978-0-8173-5931-7

Cataloging-in-Publication data is available from the Library of Congress.
ISBN-13: 978-0-8173-1598-6

Contents

★ Illustrations ★

Black-and-White Gallery

Color Gallery

★Family Notes and Acknowledgements★

We have always derived a lot of pleasure from being the granddaughters of Tasia and Bill Koikos and the nieces of Jimmy and Nicky Koikos. Our love for them comes foremost from who they were and are—Mom's loving and hilarious family. But apart from their personal attractions, who can deny the glamor of walking into a big, bustling restaurant and having the bosses stop what they're doing just to greet you? Or the almost-famous feeling we get when someone discovers, "*You're* related to the Bright Star? Wow!" We have used the Bright Star as an extension of our own homes, entertaining old friends and impressing out-of-towners with this treasure tucked away in Bessemer, Alabama. For these blessings we feel that the first people we have to thank are our late grandparents, Bill and Tasia Koikos, and our dearly loved uncles Jimmy and Nicky Koikos for giving us such a history to chronicle.

Close on their heels come the rest of the family: our parents, John and Helen Cocoris, who are simply the best parents in the world; Dad's parents, the late Gus and Anastasia Cocoris, for taking that fateful trip to Bessemer that brought Mom and Dad together; our wonderful and supportive husbands, Hugh B. Craig IV, Myron S. Chwe, and David C. Hufham; and our children, Connie Rue and Joe Craig, John Andrew and Helen Chwe, and Anna, James, and Henry Hufham.

We've always known that the Bright Star is a special place and that our grandparents and uncles are special people. That knowledge has been affirmed by the customers and employees who have shared their good feelings about the Bright Star through letters and interviews. We thank them for taking time to help us gather information for this book, and for teaching us a lot we didn't know about our family and the Bright Star.

This is the first family history any of us has undertaken, not to mention the first writing project since college! We now understand how many people are necessary to bring an idea like this to fruition. We warmly thank the following for their indispensable help: Niki Sepsas for his wonderful writing, his guidance through the book process, and his patience with our ignorance; John D. Bonduris, Jr., whose research into his family contributed enormously, along with his wife, Fannie; Mert Byram and Chris Eiland at the Bessemer Hall of History; Anita Bice for her preservation of valuable family photos; Bob

Farley for his terrific photographs of our uncles in action; and the director of the University of Alabama Press for thinking that a book about the Bright Star was as great an idea as we did.

Putting this project together has been a labor of love in the truest sense. We hope that as well as the history of the restaurant and of Bessemer, this book conveys the amount of sheer hard work—of owners, servers, managers, porters, expediters, and chefs—that has created this century-old institution. Most of all, however, we hope that the feeling of family which the Bright Star has always maintained and which makes it a fulfilling place to be comes shining through.

Stacey Cocoris Craig
Connie Cocoris Chwe
Joanna Cocoris Hufham
August 2006

★ Tribute ★

Everyone who knows the Bright Star Restaurant in Bessemer, Alabama—and that's a lot of folks in our state—think two things about it: that it's got some of the best, most consistent food in the South, and that the friendly atmosphere is as much of a draw as the delicious Greek-style seafood and steaks. Both have kept my family and me going back over and over again to the Bright Star.

I've been enjoying the food at the Bright Star since the 1970s, when my travels around Alabama kept leading me back there to refuel and relax. It was my informal campaign headquarters when I was running for the Alabama state senate. I could sit in a back booth and take telephone calls peacefully, with the waitress serving Greek snapper or refilling my coffee the only interruptions. Those were the days when Bill and Tasia Koikos, the parents of the current owners, Jimmy and Nicky, were still a part of the Bright Star's daily functioning. Having them in the restaurant—Mr. Bill standing guard over the cash register, and Miss Tasia stopping by to chat—helped create that family environment for me when I couldn't get to my own home.

My duties as U.S. senator have taken me around the world. I've been fortunate enough to have eaten many special meals in wonderful and exotic locations, but I feel just as fortunate to have the Bright Star Restaurant waiting for me when I return home to Alabama. Here's to the next one hundred years!

Richard Shelby
U.S. Senator
May 2006

★ Tribute ★

Every once in a while—possibly only once in a lifetime—if we are really lucky we will run across a restaurant that is truly special. I've had the privilege of eating at five-star restaurants in Europe as well as here in the United States, and without question my favorite restaurant in the world is the Bright Star in Bessemer, Alabama.

When I started coaching at the University of Alabama in 1990, one of the first places I ate was the Bright Star. Jimmy Koikos, one of the sons of the original owner, and his entire staff—chefs, busboys, waitresses, and hostesses—go out of their way to make everyone feel welcome and want to make each visit special.

I cannot count the different occasions that brought me there—celebrations after an Alabama win, wedding anniversaries, birthdays, Red Elephant Meetings, or just joining friends for lunch or dinner.

Their specialty is Greek snapper, and it is unlike any I have eaten anywhere. The snapper and the outstanding onion rings make my mouth water to this day. The salads are large enough for a meal, and if you want anything unusual for dessert, you can probably find it on the menu. The waitresses are always in a festive mood, and a big ROLL TIDE is always in order.

I remember going to the Bright Star one evening in March to have dinner with some friends—Doris and Carl Knight. Recruiting season was winding down and celebrating my birthday was not high on my agenda. When we arrived, Jimmy took us to a back room, and to my surprise, a room full of people yelled, "Happy Birthday!" Some of our children had come from Texas and Tennessee; my brother and his wife had flown in from Texas; and my college roommate, Bobby Drake, was there along with Bart Starr and about fifty others.

A great meal was served and lots of stories were told. My friend Jimmy Koikos, my wife, Ruth Ann, and my secretary, Linda Knowles, had kept this a secret. Where else could you go and get that kind of meal, service, great friendship, and memories that will last a lifetime? Whenever we hear that friends are going to Alabama, we always recommend that they take a trip to Bessemer and eat at the Bright Star.

The restaurant stands on its own, but the story of a young man from Greece who had very little money and could not speak English making his way to Alabama and starting a restaurant that has thrived for more than one hundred years is a heartwarming one. His struggles, his love for his restaurant, and his love for the people of Alabama and his family is one you'll not soon forget.

Gene Stallings
University of Alabama head football coach, 1990–1996
August 2006

★ Author's Note ★

A centennial celebration is a milestone event. Reaching the magical one-hundred-year plateau is a supreme accomplishment, especially in the restaurant business. The culinary landscape of any city is constantly changing as restaurants spring up seemingly overnight and, in many cases, just as quickly close their doors. A restaurant that has survived, endured, and remained prosperous for a century has obviously discovered the secret of success.

In 2007, the Bright Star Restaurant of Bessemer, Alabama, celebrates its centennial anniversary. The event not only marks a century of serving fine food to a legion of faithful followers, but also notes one hundred years of good corporate citizenship in a city that has written a colorful chapter in the history of the industrial growth of this part of the state. The commitment to being the city's premier family-style restaurant is as strong today for the Koikos brothers as it was when Tom Bonduris first opened the doors to the Bright Star in 1907.

Being asked to coordinate the research and writing of the history of the Bright Star was both an honor and a privilege for me. My mother and father cherished the close family ties that bound them with the Koikos and Cocoris families. My mother, Christine Derzis Sepsas, often told me that some of her earliest memories were of playing with Tasia Koikos, the mother of the restaurant's present owners, in the village of Sykea in Greece's Peloponnesus region when they were children. She brought the first Christmas tree that John Cocoris and his brothers ever placed in their home in the North Highlands neighborhood of Birmingham. A generation later, I am still reminded of how deep those family roots run. I have my own special memories of riding the bus with my sister to Bessemer in the 1950s to spend the day with "Miss Tasia" at the family's home on Dartmouth Avenue. Memories linger of birthdays, holidays, and other special occasions being celebrated with dinner at the Bright Star.

I am very grateful to Jimmy and Nicky Koikos, Helen Koikos Cocoris, Stacey Cocoris Craig, Connie Cocoris Chwe, and Joanna Cocoris Hufham for allowing me to participate in the preparation of this volume. I am also very appreciative of the many hours that Stacey, Connie, and Joanna devoted to the editing of the manuscript, the interviews they conducted with staff and customers, and their collection of the letters and photographs that are an integral part of the story of the Bright Star. I hope that the reader gains an understanding of the pride that the family members have in the business that grew from the dream of an immigrant from Greece and became the lasting legacy of Bill and Tasia Koikos, a legacy that continues today through the work of their children and grandchildren.

Niki Sepsas
Birmingham, Alabama
July 2006

A CENTENNIAL CELEBRATION OF

THE BRIGHT STAR RESTAURANT

★ 1 ★
Birth of a Dream

[Debardeleben] played the business game like a hand of poker.

—*Birmingham Age*, 1886

The Stage Is Set

General Andrew Jackson, frontiersman Davy Crockett, and the army of regular soldiers and volunteers who journeyed through north-central Alabama in 1813 probably paid scant attention to the forested hills of reddish-brown earth in the region through which they passed. Theirs was a military mission whose objective was to punish the Creek Indians for attacking and burning Fort Mims on the lower Alabama River in the southern part of the state earlier that year.

Nor did the Union soldiers who campaigned in the area during the Civil War see much worth destroying. The Alabama and Chattanooga Railroad (the east-west route) and the North and South Alabama Railroad would not be built until after the war. The area suffered little damage from the federal troops; one unidentified Union general, as quoted in a synopsis of Birmingham history from the city's Convention and Visitors Bureau web site, noted that the "poor, insignificant Southern village" did not even deserve an attack.

Jackson's men and the Union troops saw only poor hill country with no navigable river; they failed to see the true wealth of the region that lay below ground. The Jones Valley area through which the armies marched lies in the midst of Alabama's mineral district with rich deposits of iron ore, coal, and limestone in close proximity to each other. The extraction of these three minerals and the forging of them into iron and steel would serve as the genesis of a metropolitan area that would be defined by heavy industry and manufacturing.

Almost six decades after Jackson and his army marched through Jones Valley, a group of visionary men sifted through the wreckage of the Confederacy to build a new city on top of this mineral wealth. On

January 26, 1871, the newly formed Elyton Land Company secured options on 4,150 acres of land at $25 per acre just east of Elyton, the tiny railroad crossing in the valley. The new community would be christened "Birmingham" after Birmingham, England, one of the principal industrial cities in the United Kingdom. The founders felt the name would reflect the industrial pulse that would bring the new city to life.

Birmingham quickly took on the character of a typical boomtown as land speculators flocked to the area in anticipation of the growth of the new city. A cholera epidemic and a Wall Street crash in 1873 almost killed the newborn city. The city persevered, however, and by the turn of the twentieth century the area's mines and glowing blast furnaces were providing jobs for hundreds of men clamoring for work.

New Faces in a New Land

The early influx of labor into the Birmingham area consisted primarily of former plantation workers looking for work, but the character of the faces and the names on the work rolls were rapidly changing. Immigrants from Europe saw the promise of a better life in the New World, and they began leaving their homelands for the economic opportunities that abounded in America. Young men from Greece were especially vulnerable to the siren song of the new country, as hard times in their homeland in the waning days of the nineteenth century were forcing many to look elsewhere for opportunities.

A war with Turkey had ended with the defeat of Greek forces in 1897. To make matters worse, many Greek farmers had lost important markets for their currant crops when France and Russia, the main buyers of currants from Greece, stopped buying the dried fruit in the late 1890s. The prospect of a brighter future in America outweighed the uncertainty of starting a new life in a new land with a new language.

A tidal wave of immigration saw nearly nine million foreigners pass into New York harbor in the early years of the twentieth century. Almost 16,000 Greeks came to the United States between 1891 and 1900. Dismal economic conditions and political instability in *patrida,* the homeland, saw that number swell tenfold during the next decade as 168,000 Greeks immigrated to U.S. shores between 1901 and 1910.

For many of these Greeks, the journey began in the crowded, fetid steerage compartments of passenger ships bobbing nauseatingly for ten to twelve days in an often stormy transatlantic crossing. After processing and health screening at Ellis Island, these pilgrims rode the ferry across New York Harbor and probably gazed in wonder at the Statue of Liberty with its promise of a new life under her torch.

The Peleta Pipeline

Peter T. Bondouris made that journey just prior to the turn of the twentieth century. Peter, who later changed the spelling of the family name to "Bonduris," arrived at Ellis Island in 1895. He had left his native village of Peleta (Pe-le-TAH) in Greece's Peloponnesus region while still a very young man for the promise of economic opportunities in the New World.

He wasted little time in seizing those opportunities. After establishing his residence in the bustling city, he began buying fruit and selling it from his own fruit stand in Manhattan. With few language skills, many early immigrants entered the food services industry in this manner. The fruit stand Bonduris operated became the pipeline through which additional members of the family and many other immigrants were funneled into New York City and other points on the map.

In 1902, Tom D. Bonduris, Peter's nephew, was one of the first to take advantage of the pipeline his uncle had created. Tom was also a native of Peleta and just fourteen years old when he arrived in the United States. The youngster took a job at his uncle's fruit stand, but he was there for only two years; a bout with pneumonia forced him to return to Greece to recover.

Young Tom returned to the United States in 1906, this time through Savannah, Georgia. He continued his journey westward to Birmingham, which was still forging its future in iron and steel. Approximately one hundred Greek immigrants were living in Birmingham by 1900. Some found work in the mines and the iron and steel mills, but most discovered they were better suited for the restaurant and food service industries. In the restaurants and lunch rooms they established, they could offer the city's weary industrial workers and miners a refreshing break from their daily grind by providing a spicy hotdog, a "meat and three," or a mug of cold beer.

Phil Gulas, a second-generation restaurateur in Birmingham, explained in an article titled "Greeks Come to Birmingham" that ran in *Old Birmingham* magazine in 1994 why many of the early Greek immigrants tended to enter the restaurant business. "Most of the Greek immigrants found it easier to get along in the food business," Gulas said. "Greeks are professional in their cooking."

Denny Kakoliris, the late proprietor of the Phoenix Café and the King's Inn in Birmingham, echoed Phil's comments in the same interview: "In Greece, everybody knew how to cook; shepherds way up in the mountains had to cook for themselves. Nine times out of ten, a Greek aboard ship went to the galley and worked. The good ones became waiters and the better ones cooked. In Birmingham, the established Greek restaurants took in the new immigrants and taught them the business by working with them as dishwashers, busboys, pot washers, and waiters."

Tom Bonduris found a number of opportunities in the food service business in Birmingham when he arrived. Approximately 125 business establishments were owned by Greek Americans in the city in the early twentieth century. Tom landed a job baking pies at a restaurant called the Bright Star in the western part of Birmingham. As a new resident, the eighteen-year-old also became active in the Greek community that was forming in Birmingham and became a charter member of Chapter Three of the American Hellenic Educational Progressive Association (AHEPA), which was helping Greek immigrants assimilate into American life.

Bonduris would stay in his new home, however, for only one year before moving to the western outskirts of Jefferson County to where another town had just been born of the same industrial boom that was shaping Birmingham. Bonduris was destined to open his own business in a town that had been founded only ten years earlier by another energetic pioneer who shared Bonduris's passion for achieving the American dream.

From "Brooklyn" to "Bessemer"

Henry Fairchild Debardeleben had been born on a cotton farm in Autauga County, Alabama, in 1841. He was the great-grandson of a Hessian mercenary who had fought against the colonists during the Revolutionary War. Debardeleben's father died when he was only ten years old, and the young boy was taken in by Daniel Pratt, one of Alabama's early industrialists. After his service in the American Civil War, Debardeleben married Pratt's daughter, Ellen.

A passage in James Walker's *Things Remembered: Stories about West Jefferson County, Alabama* describes young Debardeleben as an "energetic, restless, impatient, and athletic man who could leap to mount his horse from the ground." That energy would serve him well. Under the tutelage of his father-in-law, Debardeleben expanded his horizons, working as a teamster boss, a lumberyard foreman, and a supervisor of Pratt's cotton gin.

Recognizing the tremendous potential the Jefferson County area had for industrial growth, Debardeleben and his father-in-law in 1872 acquired controlling interest in the Red Mountain Iron and Coal Company, later named the Eureka Mining Company. Six years later, he joined two other partners in reorganizing an existing company into the Pratt Coal and Coke Company, where he would serve as president. Debardeleben also acquired mineral rights to a tract of land on Red Mountain.

In 1886, he offered $100,000 for a site consisting of 4,040 acres of land located about thirteen miles southwest of Birmingham near that Red Mountain iron ore seam. Believing that the future of the area would hinge on its ability to develop its resources and become a center of industry, Debardeleben planned to build his city around eight new blast furnaces served by additional railroads. His grandiose scheme was pronounced "solid from the ground up" by the *Birmingham Age* in March 1886. The paper noted that Debardeleben "played the business game like a hand of poker," and quoted him as saying,

"We are going to build a city solid from the bottom and establish it on a rock financial basis. No stockholder will be allowed in who can't make smoke. It will take $100,000 to come in and the man who can make the most smoke can have the most stock."

Debardeleben originally named his new city Brooklyn. He changed the name to Bessemer, however, in honor of Henry Bessemer, the British scientist who developed the process for the inexpensive mass production of steel.

The young man's dream had been launched. By 1887, the new boomtown was attracting attention in newspapers around the country. The Louisville and Nashville Railroad ran a special excursion from Birmingham to Bessemer for a group of nationally known VIPs, including Robert Todd Lincoln, the late president's son. In one week alone, the Georgia Pacific Railroad sold 569 one-way tickets to Bessemer.

Debardeleben's new town soared into prominence from its inception. Land values skyrocketed as new manufacturing operations opened. Lots that in 1886 were selling for $10 to $25 per acre were bringing as much as $18,000 per acre a year later. In little more than a year, the new city recorded a population of more than 4,000, and by 1890 Bessemer was the fourth largest city in Alabama.

The nationwide panic and subsequent depression were felt in Bessemer as they were throughout the country, but the slowdown was short lived. The census of 1900 recorded approximately 10,000 people living within two miles of the city's central business district.

Economic opportunities abounded for people willing to work to achieve their dreams. William Long, who had made his way to Bessemer in 1887, partnered with Isaac Lewis to transform Long's former cornice and metalwork shop into the Long-Lewis Hardware Company. Louis Napoleon Ball, a former police chief in Tuscaloosa, opened the Bank Saloon, billed as "a palatial pleasure resort." Sam Stein built a clothing business and his son, Jake, was the first Jewish boy born in Bessemer. Savario Romano grew his small grocery store into a brick building that occupied an entire city block.

The city in which Tom Bonduris decided to put down roots was again experiencing phenomenal growth when he arrived in 1907. Early records show that there were 209 commercial establishments in Bessemer's bustling downtown, including 46 grocery stores, 6 drugstores, 15 saloons, and 6 meat markets.

The Debardeleben Coal and Iron Company had been mining thousands of tons of coal and producing pig iron in its blast furnaces since the late 1880s. Woodward Iron Company alone was running 150 beehive ovens producing coke for manufacturing steel. The Bessemer Rolling Mills plant, which occupied a twelve-acre site between Second and Fifth avenues and Twenty-Second and Twenty-Fourth streets, employed 700 to 800 men and was considered the largest in the South and one of the best-appointed in the country. U.S. Cast Iron Pipe and Foundry was producing 200 tons of pipe per day.

Several grand and elegant hotels were operating in town, offering lodging to investors arriving from as far away as England, Nova Scotia, Wales, and Australia. The Alabama Great Southern Railroad and the Louisville and Nashville Railroad brought most people into the city, while three other lines handled the bulk of hauling iron ore from the mines to the furnaces. The iron ore mines of Tennessee Coal and Iron Company, Sloss Steel and Iron Company, Woodward Iron Company, and others operated around the clock. In addition to *The Bessemer,* the first permanent newspaper in town, nine other local newspapers reported the events of the remarkable young city.

Bonduris was quick to recognize the need for a restaurant to serve the people who worked in these and the many other manufacturing and commercial operations in what was being called the "Marvel City." He wasted little time in filling that need.

One African American man born in Florence, Alabama, helped write a colorful chapter in the city's early growth. W. C. Handy had graduated from college in 1892, but was offered only $25 per month to teach school in Birmingham. He opted instead to live in Bessemer, where he earned $1.85 per day working in one of the city's pipe shops during the day, and picked up a few dollars playing with a local brass band in one of the busy saloons at night. Handy eventually made his way to St. Louis and became internationally known as the "Father of the Blues."

The "Star" Begins to Shine

Tom Bonduris invested his savings in a small restaurant with a horseshoe-shaped bar on First Avenue and Twenty-First Street in downtown Bessemer in 1907. The documents recording this transaction have been lost, but it appears that the restaurant had been owned by a man named Andrews. Bonduris's sign over the door read "The Bright Star Café," taken presumably from the restaurant that he had worked for in Birmingham.

It is not known if Bonduris ever visited New Orleans, but it appears that the restaurant he opened in Bessemer had much of the character of a French Quarter–type establishment. Early accounts indicate that the Bright Star's ceiling fans, tile floors, mirrored and marbled walls, and marble countertops were reminiscent of many of the restaurants and oyster bars of New Orleans during that time.

The original Bright Star Café had a dark tile mosaic floor inlaid with a white rosette pattern. Skinny iron barstools faced a horseshoe-shaped counter. There were no tables or booths. Behind the bar, a long, cloth-draped shelf held wine and Coca-Cola bottles, pyramids of cans, and glasses. On the wall above the

First Bright Star location at First Avenue and Twenty-First Street, 1907. Tom D. Bonduris is behind the counter. (Courtesy of the Koikos family.)

shelf, a menu was posted. A number of advertising posters were hung on the side walls. The counter consisted of a glass case containing numerous boxes of cigars.

Former Bessemer resident Robert Kachelhofer, Jr., shared his family's memories of the early Bright Star. He wrote, "Around the turn of the twentieth century, my grandfather, George L. (Boss) Bell, ran a livestock business on First Avenue and Nineteenth Street in Bessemer. He had a livestock lot on the corner of Twentieth Street and First Avenue. My mother, Margaret (Sue) Bell Kachelhofer, told me that many times she would come to the Bright Star as a child and would sit in her daddy's lap for lunch at the restaurant."

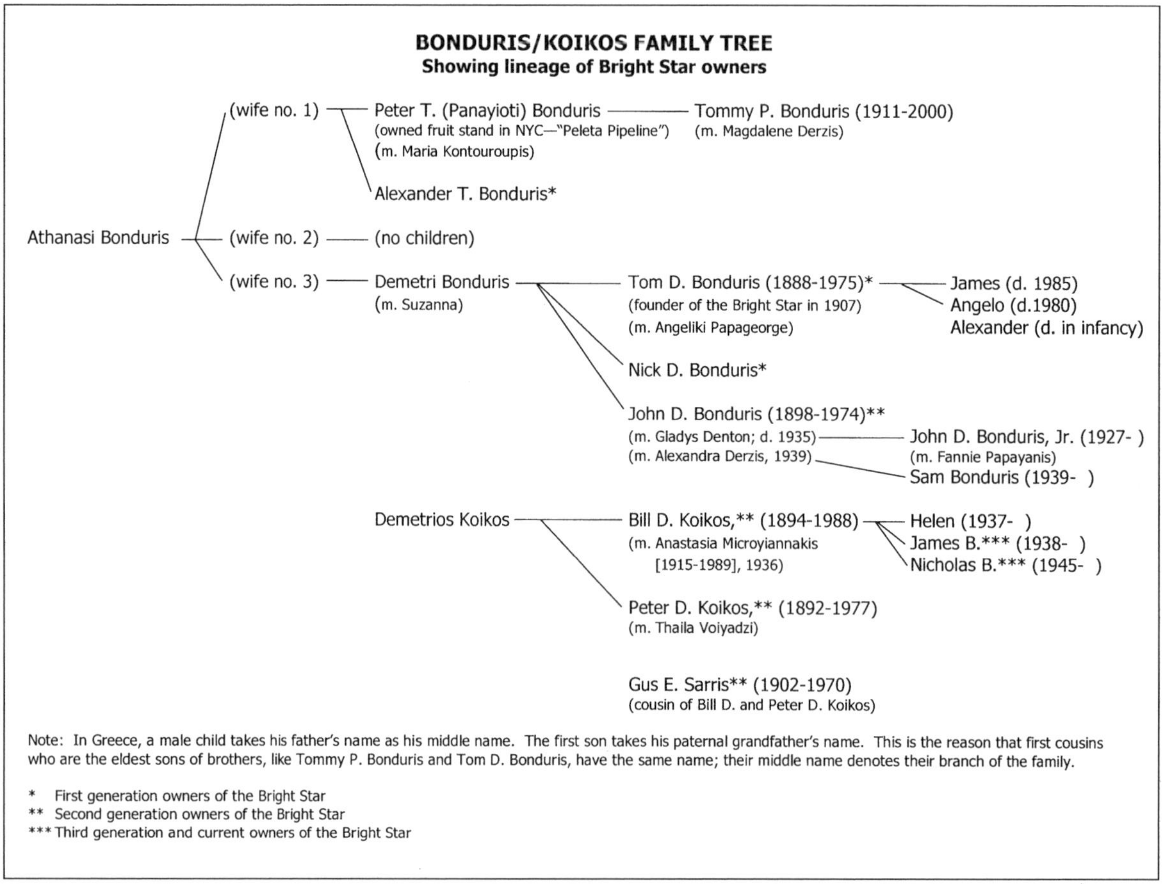

Bonduris/Koikos family tree. (Courtesy of John D. Bonduris, Jr.)

Bonduris's restaurant was by no means the first ethnic enterprise launched in the young town. Italian immigrant Mike Romano had opened a produce house in the tiny railroad settlement in 1881, six years before Bessemer was even chartered as a town. Later, another of his countrymen, Giovanni di Biago, opened the first restaurant in the area on Carolina Avenue. Bessemer's Italian immigrants would go on to own many of the small neighborhood grocery and community stores that were operating in the city in the early twentieth century.

In 1907, the "Peleta Pipeline" that had been created by Tom Bonduris's uncle Peter in New York City succeeded in bringing additional family members to Bessemer. A cousin, John N. Bonduris, arrived in

Prohibition rally, Third Avenue, Bessemer, 1907. (Courtesy of the Koikos family.)

New York City and began working at his uncle Peter's fruit stand. He eventually followed the family trail south, arriving in Bessemer in 1910.

Another cousin from Peleta, nineteen-year-old Peter D. Koikos, made the long transatlantic voyage to New York City in 1909. Also a product of the Peter Bonduris fruit stand, Koikos worked for his uncle for two years before turning south to Bessemer in 1911.

In 1912, John N. Bonduris and Peter D. Koikos opened a restaurant across from Bessemer's post office. The Post Office Café led to John's nickname of "Post Office John." He would be known by that name until the day he died.

Change was in the wind that blew through Jefferson County at that time, and those breezes would be felt in Bessemer as well. Prohibition fever was sweeping the country and the October 29, 1907, edition of the *Birmingham News* announced the results of the wet/dry vote in the county. "Saloons ousted by majority that nears eighteen hundred," the headline proclaimed. The vote in Bessemer was 344 for prohibition and 221 against. The ban on alcohol, which would take effect on the first day of January 1909, would not apply to the City of Birmingham, which voted to retain the legal sale of alcohol.

The defeated opposition voiced their concerns over the county's future. "We hope the city may escape bankruptcy," they stated in the same *News* article. "We hope the schools will not feel the burden of the changes that must follow. The laborer and manufacturer are wounded first; the merchant next; then the property owners. We abide the consequences." The victors, on the other hand, were ecstatic. The *News* noted, "Never before in the history of the United States has a county of the magnitude of Jefferson voted out the saloon."

The victory for the Prohibitionists was, naturally, a blow to the saloons and restaurants in the greater Jefferson County area, including Bessemer, and to the miners and steelworkers who enjoyed imbibing after the rigors of their work. Of course, many of Bessemer's restaurants continued to serve alcohol through "back door" or "under the counter" sales. The Bright Star was no exception; the fledgling business could not afford to lose customers. As Nicky Koikos, a descendant of Tom D. Bonduris and present co-owner of the Bright Star, related, "During Prohibition, people would ask to be served a 'toddy' in coffee cups. Tom Bonduris often obliged them."

A Region on the Move

The same rapid growth and expansion that were making Bessemer the "Marvel City" were fast transforming Birmingham into the "Magic City." The whole region was becoming known as the industrial center of the South. The Tennessee Coal and Iron Company had been purchased by U.S. Steel in 1907; the largest crowd ever to witness a baseball game in the South turned out for the inaugural game at Rickwood Field in 1910; and the twenty-two-story Jefferson County Savings Bank Building opened in downtown Birmingham in 1912 as the South's tallest skyscraper. Soon, Bessemer and Birmingham would become the heart of a great industrial district known throughout the world.

The City of Bessemer was benefiting from the meteoric growth that marked Jefferson County at the time, but the dynamic young city was making headlines in its own right. A 1902 report of Bessemer school superintendent James M. Dill, excerpted in Walker's *Things Remembered,* noted, "It is not known abroad nor fully appreciated at home that Bessemer is the only city in the State of Alabama that maintains absolutely free public schools." On the medical front, the first hospital in western Jefferson County was opened in Bessemer in 1913. The three-story building was located on Third Avenue between Seventeenth and Eighteenth streets.

The Bright Star was keeping pace with the growth of the city in which it was born. The restaurant that Tom Bonduris had opened was fast becoming known as a place to get a good meal at a reasonable price. In 1909, Tom's brother Nick D. Bonduris entered the United States through Savannah and made his way to Bessemer to work at the Bright Star. As the restaurant continued to attract a large following,

Ad from the *Birmingham News,* May 1907, advertising the "Marvel City." (Courtesy of Birmingham Public Library Archives.)

the brothers planned to move into larger quarters. Having outgrown their original location on First Avenue and Twenty-First Street, they moved in 1909 to a new location on Second Avenue and Twentieth Street.

The second Bright Star Restaurant had a dark floor, probably made of tile. The restaurant had a horseshoe-shaped bar with iron stools similar to those in the original location. Fans hung from a high plastered ceiling. The walls had a wood-paneled wainscot. Above the wainscot on the back and right-side walls were mirrors. Tucked behind a wing wall on the right side were three tables with white tablecloths that offered seating for two on wooden chairs. An iron cash register and cigar boxes sat on a wooden table behind the counter.

In 1911, it was time to move again. The third Bright Star was located on Nineteenth Street between

Second Bright Star location at Second Avenue and Twentieth Street, 1910. Tom D. Bonduris is standing behind the counter, closest to the camera. (Courtesy of the Koikos family.)

Second and Third avenues. The restaurant had a mosaic tile floor with a diamond pattern against a white background. A high plastered ceiling held the ubiquitous ceiling fans. The left side of the restaurant featured a long bar. Square tables seating four or five guests each were placed along the right wall. These tables featured white tablecloths, wooden chairs, and upright, folded napkins. The restaurant featured the same wooden wainscot and mirrors as did its predecessor. A wooden post in the middle of the room divided the bar area from the tables. Old-fashioned iron coat racks with curved hooks stood alongside the tables. Cloth-covered shelves behind the bar held liquor bottles, cloth sacks of coffee, and glasses. A coffee urn sat at the far end.

Third Bright Star location on Nineteenth Street between Second and Third avenues, 1913. Tom D. Bonduris stands at the far right. (Courtesy of the Koikos family.)

The downtown district of Bessemer had grown considerably from the city's original little cluster of businesses facing the Southern Railway tracks on Alabama and Carolina avenues. As the central business district moved steadily away from the tracks, the Bonduris brothers made certain that their Bright Star restaurant remained in the heart of the city's bustling commercial and industrial activity. Their location gave the restaurant a unique position in the center of what had become some of the choicest real estate in the city.

The Berney Brothers Bank Building on the northeast corner of Second Avenue and Nineteenth Street was hailed at the turn of the century as "the neatest, prettiest, most artistic and elaborate architecturally of any construction in Bessemer." Second and Nineteenth was also the location of the Grand Hotel, one of the early city's finest, which William Berney had built for $60,000. Adjoining the bank on Second Avenue, the Adler Block was the first large brick block completed in Bessemer. The Charleston Block on Second Avenue and Nineteenth Street was a magnificent structure with fronts of pressed brick, marble, and iron. *The Bessemer* sang its praises. "It is an elaborate piece of work that would be creditable to a city of half a million inhabitants," the paper proclaimed. "There is hardly a city in the South that can boast of construction superior to it."

Reports of the many economic opportunities in the Jefferson County area continued to drift back across the Atlantic to the Greeks' *patrida.* These stories of a better life for those willing to work hard induced a third Bonduris brother, John D., to leave the village of Peleta in 1914 and make his way to New York City. It was not long before the sixteen-year-old arrived in Bessemer, where he joined his brothers, Tom and Nick, at the Bright Star.

He was part of a tremendous surge in immigration to the United States from Greece and a proportionate swelling of the number of Greek Americans settling in Jefferson County. By 1910 there were 302 Greek immigrants living in Birmingham, making it one of the largest Greek communities in the South. A decade later that number had jumped to 485.

John D. Bonduris's arrival in America and settling in Bessemer could not have been at a more fortuitous time. The storm clouds that had been gathering over Europe were about to burst and plunge the world into a war of unprecedented proportions. Greece would again be the scene of bitter fighting, and, in its aftermath, more of its sons and daughters would seek better lives in the United States.

Berney Brothers Bank Building, ca. 1918. (Courtesy of the Bessemer Hall of History.)

★2★

The Dream Becomes Reality

I was very happy to come to this country.
—Bill Koikos

A World at War

The skies over Europe in 1914 were filled with dark and ominous clouds of war. The Balkan Wars of 1912–13 threatened to expand and create a global conflagration.

The spark that ignited the powder keg proved to be the assassination of Archduke Ferdinand of Austria-Hungary in Sarajevo, Serbia, in June 1914. The outbreak of hostilities against Serbia was quickly followed by additional declarations of war from across Europe as the web of entangling alliances resulted in a global conflict.

Britain, France, and Russia formed the Triple Entente and squared off against the Central Powers of Germany, Austria-Hungary, and Turkey. The ensuing war would have a huge impact on the growth of the Greek community in Jefferson County.

Between a Rock and a Hard Place

The declaration of war in Europe put the Greek government in a precarious position. King Constantine's wife, Queen Sofia, was the sister of Kaiser Wilhelm of Germany. The king, naturally, leaned toward neutrality in the conflict, but opposition forces under Prime Minister Eleftherios Venizelos pushed for entry on the side of the Allies. The supporters of the monarchy and those of Venizelos very nearly led Greece into civil war.

Realizing the strategic importance of Greece, the Allies pushed even harder for the Greek army to join the war on their side and bolster their forces in eastern Europe. The entry of Bulgaria, traditionally a foe of Greece, into the conflict as a Central Power further intensified the call for Greece to enter the war on

Though these three Bonduris relatives—Tom D., Nick D., and Alexander T.—are known as the first-generation owners of the Bright Star, they may not have been business partners in the usual sense of the term.

The late Tommy P. Bonduris, son of Peter T. and cousin of Tom D. Bonduris, stated in an interview that these three co-owned the restaurant as equal partners. However, Tommy P.'s wife, Magdalene Derzis Bonduris, has clarified more recently that rather than making them partners, Tom Bonduris provided a stable and profitable position for Nick and Alexander in his business as long as they remained in the United States. She asserts that when Nick and Alexander returned to Greece, they had earned enough money working at the Bright Star to begin comfortable lives for themselves and their families. In the tradition of his uncle Peter, Tom D. Bonduris used his business to provide employment for his newly arrived relatives. They, in turn, were a source of dependable labor and moral support. Their partnership was based on a desire to help each other succeed.

the side of the Allies. Great Britain eventually imposed a blockade on Greece to force it to enter the offensive against the Central Powers. For 106 days, near-famine conditions existed in southern Greece as virtually no goods moved into or out of Greek ports.

In 1916, the fall of Macedonia to the Central Powers convinced the Greeks that despite their mixed emotions, alliances, and royal family ties, they had no choice but to declare war. Their declaration in June 1917 came just two months after the United States declared war on the Central Powers. Approximately 70,000 Greeks fought on behalf of the Allied effort in World War I.

The Star Continues to Shine

Greek immigration to the United States almost completely halted during the war. The flood of immigration that had poured 450,000 Greeks into America between 1890 and 1915 quickly dried up. Never again would those numbers reach the almost 25,000 Greek immigrants per year who came to America during the late nineteenth and early twentieth centuries.

One Greek who did arrive on these shores during that period, however, was another member of the Bonduris family from Peleta. Alexander T. Bonduris, an uncle of Tom D. and Nick D. Bonduris, made his way to New York City and, via his brother Peter's fruit stand, went on to Bessemer, arriving in 1915. He immediately began work at the Bright Star.

In May 1915, the Bondurises moved their business into its fourth location, the newly completed Realty Building on Nineteenth Street between Third and

Completed Realty Building, ca. 1920. Note the sign reading "Bright Star Café" at street level on the far right. (Courtesy of Bessemer Hall of History.)

Fourth avenues. Built by the Bessemer Realty Company, the four-story building was home to Pope Drugstore, Realty Barbershop, and several legal and medical offices. The building was very modern for its day, boasting two elevators, a steam heating system, and an elegant lobby. A poolroom was located in the basement.

Also at the restaurant was another cousin, Constantine "Gus" Sarris, who had left Greece in 1915 when he was thirteen years old and emigrated to Bessemer. Sarris claimed to have laid the last brick in the kitchen of the new Bright Star so it could open at its fourth location in the Realty Building.

Those Famous Murals

One special touch that went into the decoration of the 1915 Bright Star still impresses today. A series of

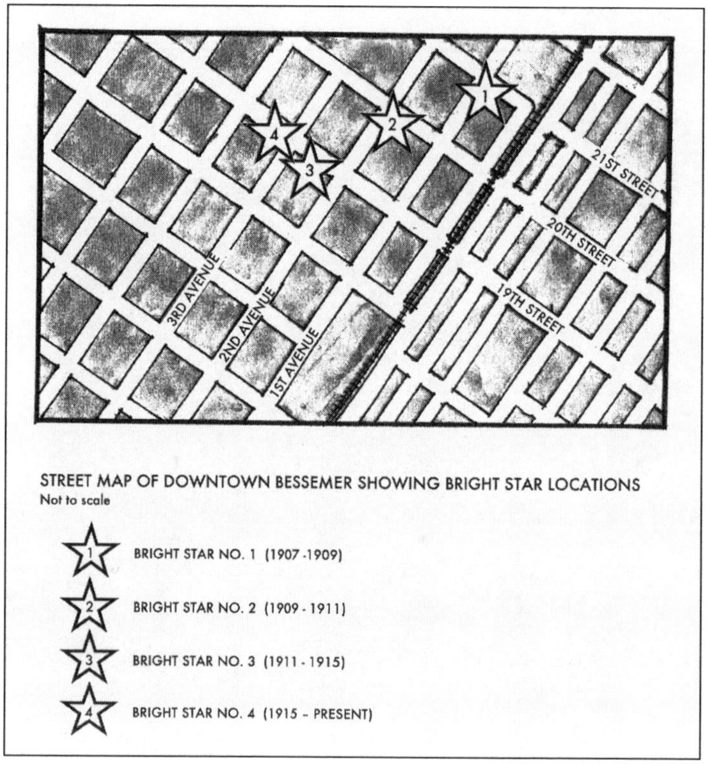

Street map of downtown Bessemer showing all four locations of the Bright Star. (Courtesy of Connie Cocoris Chwe.)

scenic murals was mounted on the walls of the Bright Star shortly after it opened in the Realty Building. The story of how they came to be was contributed by Mrs. Fleta Edwards of Tuscaloosa, Alabama, and was written by her father, Jim Morton Montgomery, in 1999. The account was based on the reminiscences of his ninety-seven-year-old mother, Mrs. Sidney Morton Montgomery.

"Ninety years or so ago, a traveling artist was hired by the Bright Star Café to decorate their walls with paintings," Mrs. Montgomery explained.

> He was from Germany, so the scenes he painted are imaginary views of his country. That's a little odd, because the owners were originally from Greece, and the menu almost a century later still has many Greek dishes.
>
> Rather than have the artist paint while diners were eating, they looked for a place he could paint and bring the canvases to paste on the wall. Across the street was my grandfather's store, Morton Hardware Company. Behind the store were long sheds where lumber and other supplies were stored. To help his

restaurant owner neighbors, Grandfather offered the shed as a temporary studio for the artist. Apparently, the art was so interesting they moved the canvases to the front store windows so passersby could glimpse his work, too.

Jimmy Koikos, who with his brother, Nicky, currently owns and operates the Bright Star, discussed the murals in a 2004 interview for a compilation of oral histories of the local Greek community titled "Greeks in Birmingham." "These murals have been up there since 1915, when they were painted by an itinerant artist," Jimmy said. "He drank a lot, but he had talent. So he painted one mural and Mr. Bonduris liked it so he painted all European scenes one by one and put them up. They fed him and wined him and he just wandered on through. He never dreamed they'd be up here ninety years later."

Fourth Bright Star location, 1915. Note the murals around the walls, the coffee urns at the center back, and the cash register at front right. (Courtesy of the Koikos family.)

Over the decades, the murals have been preserved mainly by being revarnished whenever the restaurant's original plaster walls were repainted. However, by the 1970s, the plaster behind the murals was beginning to disintegrate. Mary Frances Cull is a Bessemer resident whose brother-in-law, Earl Cull, worked with Jack Costello, a local painting contractor. Mrs. Cull, in an interview with Costello's widow, related that at that time Costello and Cull carefully stabilized the crumbling plaster by applying glue through a hypodermic syringe. They then cleaned the varnished surfaces gently with soap and water. The ninety-two-year-old murals still glow today down the length of the restaurant, a testament to the skill of an unknown artist.

A Soldier from Peleta

Greece suffered greatly during the Balkan Wars and World War I, and few opportunities existed for the thousands of discharged veterans who were returning to the small villages that had sent them off to defend their country.

Peleta was no exception. The village is situated on a plateau almost 2,300 feet above sea level in the Arcadia prefecture and the Kynouria province of Greece's Peloponnesus region. A farming village of traditional stone houses and a few coffee shops, Peleta was popular as the spot where farmers brought their wheat to be ground into flour. Dotted with stately fir and cedar trees and surrounded by the Parnon mountains, the pastoral setting was peaceful and idyllic, but offered little to attract a young man who wanted to create a future for himself.

Vasilios (Bill) Koikos was a native of Peleta and had been apprenticed to a baker on the island of Hydra at the age of twelve. He recalled to his daughter Helen that he slept in a loft above the bakery and awoke to smell of bread baking. He was lonely but accepted his fate to be away from his family in order to learn a trade. Later, Koikos was among the thousands who served in the Greek army during World War I. Born in 1894, he was twenty years old when he entered the military in 1914. He served until his discharge five years later.

The Koikos home, like most others in Peleta, was made of stone, as wood was, and still is, a premium commodity in Greece. Most of the country's forests were denuded centuries ago, and builders relied on reinforced concrete for most dwellings and other buildings. Owners would whitewash their homes each Easter with quicklime to give the houses a new look during the holiest days in the Greek Orthodox religion.

The Koikos home was a one-story stone dwelling with a tile roof. A low stone wall surrounding the home had a metal gate that invited the visitor into a small courtyard shaded by the ubiquitous grape arbors that adorn most Greek farm homes. Next to the entrance to the house was another traditional

Eleni and Demetrios Koikos, parents of Bill and Pete Koikos, ca. 1927. Demetrios raised wheat, beans, okra, squash, and tomatoes for a living. (Courtesy of the Koikos family.)

Greek home appliance—the outdoor wood-burning oven. Its beehive shape, unchanged over centuries, radiated heat evenly for perfect cooking.

A single door opened into the living area, measuring roughly forty by twenty feet, that was centered on a stone fireplace. An iron hook mounted on the inside wall perpetually held a pot or pan. The fireplace not only provided a place for inside cooking but was the single source of heat during the cold winters in the mountains of the Peloponnesus.

Along a side wall were built-in storage bins, called *kanape,* that occupied about half of the wall space and had hinged lids. Inside, the family stored legumes, wheat, and other dried goods. The bins were also used as beds for the four Koikos children—Bill, Pete, Nick, and Candio.

The other side wall was a partition that separated the living area from a storage area of about fifteen by twenty feet where hay was kept. This area also served as quarters for the family's mules. A farmer had little qualms about sharing his quarters with his mules, which ranked among his most prized possessions. His mules not only plowed his fields, but provided transportation on the rocky trails that connected the various villages scattered among the rugged mountains of the region.

The Koikos home had no electricity and relied on a well for water. About forty or fifty yards behind the home was the outhouse, simply a hole in the ground with a wooden platform built over it.

A second story was added to the home in 1927, the same year that Bill's brother Peter D. Koikos returned to Greece to marry Thalia Voiyadzi. In 1990, Tassos Koikos, a nephew of Bill Koikos, undertook another renovation. Jimmy Koikos is justifiably proud of the fact that he has slept in the home in which his father was born in 1895.

After his discharge from the Greek army in 1919, Bill returned to his home in Peleta but decided to turn toward America and follow the pipeline that several of his relatives had accessed to build a new life.

Bill left his home in the mountains and traveled twenty-two miles to Leonidion, a town of about 4,000 people and the capital of the province of Kynouria. From there, a train took him to Athens, where he boarded a steamship bound for New York City. Continuing his journey to Bessemer, he arrived on June 15, 1920. "My brother, Pete, was already here," Bill said in an interview videotaped by Matt Zarna in 1986 for his production of *Legacy: A Living History of Greek Immigrants in Birmingham.* "He sent money for my fare so I could come, too. I was very happy to come to this country. The hardest thing for me to get used to was the language. We didn't have much chance for education in Greece."

The boomtown that was Bill's new home was particularly intriguing, especially for a young man from a small farm village. "I liked it very much," Bill reminisced in a 1984 interview with Gaynell Morrow for Bessemer's hometown newspaper, the *Western Star.* "Only one street light, very dark, brick street on Nineteenth Street, dirt on others." He was not particularly concerned about the condition of the streets, however. "I didn't care what the streets were made of," he said with a laugh in a 1980 interview published in the *Birmingham News* that was written by family friend Dennis Washburn.

> Brick or cobblestone, I couldn't say either word in English. And they weren't as bad as the dirt roads they had in the little Greek town where I grew up. There weren't many cars to be seen on the streets back then. Maybe just a few Model T Fords and there were a few horses and buggies still around. Most people used the streetcars in moving around the city.
>
> Bessemer was booming back then because of mining and iron and steel making. Anybody who wanted to work could find a job. The pay wasn't very much. Nothing at all like it is today.

Bill immediately went to work with his brother Pete and cousin Tom Bonduris at the Bright Star. Life was exciting for the young man, and learning the language and adapting to the customs of his adopted home were sometimes amusing. Working as a busboy and an eager waiter, Bill once greeted a customer who came in the door rubbing his hands on a particularly cold winter day. Commenting that it was "pretty chilly" outside, the customer was reportedly startled when Bill raced to the kitchen and returned with a bowl of chili for him.

"The restaurant, it was most beautiful," Bill continued in the same *Western Star* interview. "Very cheap, everything very cheap. It was thirty-five cents for a vegetable plate. A big bowl of soup was ten and fifteen cents, a cup of coffee with doughnut five cents. Steaks were only sixty-five or seventy-five cents each. And we sold beef stew, oysters, catfish, and chicken. It was a funny thing but chickens were very high then. Not many people ate chicken. The only chickens I could get were brought in to me from people living in the country."

Bill Koikos at first lived off the tips he earned waiting and bussing tables at the Bright Star. He told his son Nicky that during his breaks, he would often go down to a nearby park for a quick nap on one of the benches there. He sent most of his wages to his mother in Greece to enable her to provide suitable marriage dowries for his sisters.

"I was working for $40 a month, and I sent all the money I made to my mother in Greece," Bill commented in 1980 in an interview in the *Birmingham News.*

> My father was dead and there were six brothers and four sisters (some half siblings) to support. Things were very bad in Greece then and some of my brothers and sisters died very early. Here at the Bright Star we were open about twenty hours a day. All the people working in the restaurant were men or boys. We didn't have any girls working here. The reason I could send all my salary home was we used to get little tips sometimes—a nickel, dime, or quarter. Sometimes we even got a half-dollar. This was the money I used to live on and buy a few clothes.

Bill lived at the local YMCA with Tommy P. Bonduris, the son of Peter T. Bonduris. "I was born in New York City in 1911," Tommy explained in an interview for *Legacy.* "We moved back to Greece when I was eight years old. I came back to America and to Bessemer in 1927 where I worked as a busboy and waiter at the Bright Star. A plate lunch at the restaurant in those days went for twenty-five cents. You got a meat, three vegetables, dessert, and a drink. Coffee and three doughnuts was a nickel. We worked

Ad from Bessemer High School *Kallista,* 1915. (Courtesy of Bessemer Hall of History.)

twelve to fourteen hours a day, usually seven days a week. Bill Koikos and I roomed together at the YMCA in Bessemer for ten dollars a month."

The Bessemer of their day continued to throb with excitement and energy.

"We had a lot of people in Bessemer back in those days," said James O. Cain, who celebrated his one-hundredth birthday on May 19, 2006, and recalled much of his life in Bessemer in a 2005 interview.

> It was a wonderful place to grow up. We used to come down here on Saturday afternoon, park our car in front of Kress's [Department Store], and we would sit there for an hour or so just watching people. You would come and sit in the cars and eat dinner right there. You wouldn't go back home until night.
>
> Money was money back in those days. I could take five dollars and go to the grocery store and buy a lot of groceries. Bessemer had plenty of people in it. Everybody was working and everything was good. We used to have a grocery store on every corner. There were four movie theaters in Bessemer in those days. There used to be bar rooms here, saloons on every corner.

> There was even a place where you could go and get a little lovin'. They had a cathouse on Freeman Street and Carolina Avenue. All the miners got paid on Friday and [would] come and spend their money at the cathouse. Well, they weren't making but about two or three dollars a day over there in the mines. By the time they [bought] their groceries and [paid] the water bill and the house rent and everything out of it they wouldn't have but a dollar or two left and they would come to town and get them a beer and a haircut and then they were broke and had to go back home.

Mitch Abercrombie, a Bessemer native who has owned White's True Value Hardware Store down the street from the Bright Star for forty years, recounted his father's tale of the miners' leisure activities: "Many of those guys were eager to visit the 'houses of interest' that a number of 'madams' operated here in town. Some of the miners went straight there before going anyplace else. They were often still covered in coal dust. It was often said that some of those 'ladies of interest' would have blond hair on Friday afternoons, but their hair was coal black on Monday mornings."

A meal at the Bright Star, even back in the 1920s, was a special occasion for many people in Bessemer and the surrounding communities. Mr. Cain, who operated a barbershop in Bessemer for almost seventy-five years, recalled his first meal at the city's popular restaurant. "My first meal I got to eat at the Bright Star was a Christmas Eve dinner in 1928," he noted. "My brothers shut the whole barbershop down and they would bring us down here and feed us. There were about six men working there. We ate broiled snapper, a big piece of broiled snapper, for eighty-five cents. It came with a salad and potatoes on the side. I was only making four or five dollars a week and couldn't afford to come back and eat no more."

End of an Era

In 1924, with Nick and Alexander Bonduris having returned to Greece, Tom Bonduris sold his restaurant to the second generation of family members. Bill Koikos and his brother Pete joined John D. Bonduris and Gus Sarris as the new owners. In the four years that he had been in America, Bill Koikos had been so thrifty and industrious that he had saved enough money to enter into partnership with the other three men.

Tom Bonduris retired and returned to his native Greece with his wife, Angeliki Papageorge. They had lived in the house he had built on Third Avenue and Sixteenth Street across from Debardeleben Park, where Angeliki had often prepared meals for the Bright Star workers in their off hours. The couple had three children, James, Angelo, and Alexander, who died as an infant.

Upon his return to Greece, Bonduris decided that he was not quite ready for retirement. He purchased a movie theater that during the Nazi occupation of Greece during World War II became the headquarters for the German command in Athens.

Tom's sons Angelo and Jimmy, who had been born in Bessemer and New York City, respectively, boarded a steamer bound for New York City when World War II broke out in 1939. Jimmy was within three months of receiving a law degree from the University of Athens. When the United States entered the war in 1941, Jimmy enlisted in the army, where he operated a tank in the Seventh Armored Division and participated in the Battle of the Bulge. Angelo graduated with a degree in chemistry from the University of Alabama before joining the Army Air Corps, where he served as a pharmacist.

Tom D. Bonduris, the founder of the Bright Star Restaurant, died in 1975. His wife died a few years later. Though he had left Bessemer fifty years before, Bonduris's obituary appeared in the Bessemer section of the *Birmingham News* on December 11, 1975. It stated that, in addition to his achievement as a restaurateur, he had been the first Greek member of the Bessemer Masons and had become a Shriner.

Second-Generation Restaurant

The Bright Star that the new owners purchased in 1924 was a far cry from the horseshoe-shaped bar and stools of the original restaurant. Along the right-hand side, a long counter with a marble shelf above it ran the length of the space. A series of back booths had been added where customers could eat in a private, intimate setting. The cashier's counter bristled with packages of cigarettes. A four-foot-high glass jar, reputedly a turn-of-the-century advertising gimmick filled with the H. J. Heinz Company's "57 varieties," greeted customers at the entrance to the restaurant. It is still at the restaurant today.

And there were the famous chrome coffee urns, recalled John D. Bonduris, Jr., son of owner John D. Bonduris.

> The Bright Star was known at the time for its coffee and the doughnuts that Gus Sarris made. The large, sugar-coated doughnuts were beautiful in their own right. When the customers came in, the first things they admired were the [Heinz 57] jar and the coffee urns. The urns were outstanding items and the Bright Star took pride in them and kept them spotless. They were very prominently displayed, three across. The center one, which held water, was slightly higher than the other two, which held coffee. They were always kept very clean, and I think that was one of the reasons their coffee was so good.

Those urns were still noteworthy in the 1950s, as Bessemer native Will Simmons recalled: "I started coming [to the Bright Star] as a nine-year-old boy with my dad, who delivered bread here for Home Baking Company. The most frightening things to me were the big coffee urns. They were big, shiny things in the back. For a nine-year-old, they were pretty impressive. Mr. Bill and Mr. Pete would climb up a ladder to clean them."

John D. Bonduris, Jr., described other prominent features of the 1920s restaurant.

> An item that you might have noticed in the Bright Star at that time was the skylight. The skylight was in the same location as the urns . . . [and on] a beautiful sunny day it gave more illumination into the Bright Star, showed off its interior and was very pleasant. I think the environment really helped with enjoying the food.
>
> Another noteworthy characteristic was the cleanliness of the Bright Star. The tile floors were kept spotless, clean and mopped, but they would put a fine layer of sawdust over the tile floor for safety reasons. After it dried, of course, they would remove it. There were white tablecloths and flowers on each table.
>
> At the far end of the counter, near the front, was a large iron cash register. Its silver color lent some decoration to the front of the restaurant. It was later moved to the very front of the Bright Star to sit atop a display case full of cigars.
>
> Around the very front were large windows that not only let in more light but, during the Christmas and Easter seasons, allowed you to look out across Nineteenth Street and see the decorated windows of the shops. The atmosphere of the seasons was very evident.
>
> At the back corner of the restaurant was an entranceway into the lobby of the Realty Building. It was a quick and easy way to get to the barbershop through that little door, very convenient to customers coming in and out through there.
>
> These points are indicative of the people who ran the place and their emphasis on cleanliness. Their goal was to please the public, and they focused on how things looked.

Memorable Moments

It was during Bessemer's heyday of the 1920s that the Bright Star became known as the place where memories were made. People gathered to eat and families celebrated special events.

Longtime Bright Star customer Margaret Ann Griffin wrote, "On her sixteenth birthday, July 10, 1924, my mother, Margaret Elizabeth, was honored with lunch by her parents, Pearl and Frank Turner, at the Bright Star, an exciting restaurant in the City of Bessemer. My grandparents owned a dairy farm outside of town and were very busy and confined. In those days, to dine out in a restaurant was a special treat. To leave four brothers at home and dine alone with her parents was a memorable occasion for my mother. Throughout the years, whenever she dined at the Bright Star, she always recalled that special day."

Another special occasion was reported by a Miss Lewis, an eighty-seven-year-old Bessemer native, who recalled, "My parents, Edward and Maria Jane Lewis, were married and had their wedding dinner at the Bright Star on March 9, 1919."

Other patrons have similar memories. "My parents were married on April 22, 1924, at the old Our Lady of Sorrows Church on Avenue F," wrote Betty Jean Antonio Baldone in a letter to the Bright Star. "It was the Tuesday after Easter and the church was filled with Easter lilies and flowers. They had a beautiful wedding and reception. After that they came home to Bessemer to a small house on Sixth Avenue and Nineteenth Street. The next morning they had a wonderful wedding breakfast at the Bright Star."

And the Bright Star was the place, as James O. Cain recalled, where couples came together. "I met a girl under the clock that used to hang on the wall there," he explained. "It was love at first sight. She was there with her sister and brother-in-law. I met her over there and then I went on home and I called her on New Year's Eve. I got a date and went to see her for a little while and then we got married the following year. We were married for fifty-nine years when she died."

Roaring through the Twenties

The United States raced through the 1920s with gusto. The war had ended, the economy was strong, and the papers were filled with headlines touting the heady times of the day: the 1925 Scopes "Monkey" Trial in Dayton, Tennessee, in which John Thomas Scopes was fined $100 for teaching the theory of evolution; Charles Lindbergh made the first transatlantic solo flight in 1927; and Al Jolson revolutionized the motion picture industry in 1927 with the first "talkie," *The Jazz Singer.*

The economic boom that was sweeping the nation during the 1920s had its counterpart in Bessemer. In 1921, the Chickasaw Shipbuilding and Car Company, a subsidiary of the Tennessee Coal and Iron Corporation (TCI), built its first steel railroad car in Fairfield, Alabama. Eight years later, TCI sold some of its Chickasaw building and equipment to Pullman Standard for a new plant to be constructed on a hundred-acre tract of land in Bessemer. The new plant would be just east of town on a deserted site that had been formerly occupied by blast furnaces, piles of slag, and beehive coke ovens.

A huge Southern barbecue served to some three hundred visitors, railroad executives, and Bessemer and Birmingham civic leaders marked the opening of the Pullman plant in 1929. In just a few months, Pullman had built and delivered six hundred boxcars for the National Railway of Mexico.

Woodward Iron Company had grown from a series of iron furnaces founded in the Bessemer area in 1881 to an industrial giant operating miles of railroad track, four locomotives, fifty railroad cars, sixty-three single coke ovens, eighty double coke ovens, and housing for more than one thousand employees. Harbison Walker Refractories opened its second brick works in Bessemer in 1925. The Bessemer Rolling Mill, operated by TCI, was running at full speed.

The hardware store of William Long and Isaac Lewis had become a fixture in town. The Bessemer Foundry and Machine Company and Krebs Manufacturing were also adding to the city's employment rolls. Three lumber yards provided building materials for the construction boom.

The old Bessemer Board of Trade, which had been organized in 1888 to promote the new city to the outside industrial and commercial world, was replaced in 1922 by the Bessemer Chamber of Commerce (now the Bessemer Area Chamber of Commerce). Composed of the city's leading industrial, business, and professional people, the chamber became active in showcasing Bessemer's many attributes to prospective businesses.

The population of Bessemer had almost doubled from 10,846 in 1910 to 18,674 in 1920. Just five years later, it had jumped by another 44 percent to 26,894.

Bessemer's manufacturing-based economy soared as it had done in no other time in its past, and the Bright Star rode the wave of prosperity, as Nicky Koikos, one of the restaurant's present owners, pointed out.

> The "Roaring Twenties" was a busy period for the Bright Star. [The Bright Star was] open twenty-four hours a day; you could buy hot homemade doughnuts in the wee hours of the morning. If a husband was "out late" in downtown Bessemer, he would come in to buy an oyster loaf as a peace offering to his disgusted wife.
>
> The modern steam heat radiators of the Realty Building provided great comfort in the cold winter months. Ceiling fans and a skylight that opened provided ventilation and some relief during the summer. The private booths provided quiet sanctuaries for parties of six to sixteen guests. Large banquets for civic and fraternal organizations were held in the dining room on tables with white tablecloths. Silver sugar bowls and creamers were on each table.
>
> The restaurant's founder, Mr. Tom Bonduris, as well as the second-generation owners, attempted to

establish a higher level of dining at the Bright Star. His white tablecloths, starched napkins, silver-plated flatware, and sugar and creamers provided guests with an elegant dining experience.

In the 1920s and 1930s, most of the servers were male. They wore starched white coats and ties.

It seemed to many that there was no end in sight to the boom times in which the city and the country reveled. The bubble, however, was about to burst. The Bright Star, like almost every business enterprise in America at that time, was about to skid into an economic depression, the likes of which the United States and the rest of the world had not known.

Banquet at the Bright Star, ca. 1919. (Courtesy of the Koikos family.)

★3★

The Depression Years and World War II

Lots of people came here hungry. I never turned them away.
—Bill Koikos

The Bubble Bursts

The boom psychology and speculative euphoria of the 1920s came to an abrupt halt in 1929. Though the economy of the United States had begun sliding into a recession in the spring of that year, it was the Wall Street crash of October 1929 that began the Great Depression. By 1933, approximately 11,000 of the 25,000 banks in the United States had been forced into insolvency.

The failure of so many banks, combined with a nationwide loss of confidence in the economy, led to much-reduced levels of spending and demand for production. By 1932, U.S. manufacturing output had fallen to 54 percent of its 1929 level. In addition, unemployment skyrocketed. Approximately seven million U.S. workers were without jobs in 1930. Two years later, unemployment had risen to 25–30 percent of the workforce.

For a city like Bessemer with an industrial pulse, the depression hit especially hard. Orders for its manufactured goods slowed and eventually stopped. In 1931, the new Pullman plant closed and would not reopen for several years. The bread lines and soup kitchens that became familiar sights across America became common in Bessemer as well.

Times of Struggle

The hard times would put the management skills of the owners of the Bright Star to a grueling test. Having purchased the restaurant just five years before the onset of the Great Depression, Bill Koikos and his partners faced an enormous challenge. In an interview recorded in 2005, John D. Bonduris, Jr., recalled that

> [during] the Great Depression of the 1930s, the Bright Star remained in business, despite the many hardships of its owners. The place continued to provide customers with white tablecloths, specially folded white napkins, and waiters in white coats. The Bright Star fell behind in rental payments to pay the realty company who owned the building at the time. The company allowed the Bright Star to pay them a percentage of their take, as they could. The arrangement helped the restaurant to stay in business. It was a case of hard work, providing quality food, and attention to service, together with good cooperation of the food vendors, that enabled the owners to continue operation. The Bright Star also stayed open during the period where no one really had anything, and many residents of Bessemer would come to the Bright Star asking for any food that they might have. The Bright Star willingly shared its food with people who were hungry and destitute.

Bill Koikos weighed in on the hard times experienced during the depression in an article that appeared in the *Birmingham News* in 1980. "It was very bad," he said. "Between 1930 and 1932, most of the banks closed. We were staying here twenty hours a day most of the time. And most of the time, we didn't even take in $20. We couldn't pay our rent and could hardly pay the light bill even though it wasn't very much. We were only making three or four dollars a week then."

The Bright Star's famous doughnuts became more than just a tasty addition to a cup of coffee during those days. Two doughnuts for a nickel became a meal for many who could afford little more. John D. Bonduris, Jr., recalled,

> People would come to the management and ask if they had anything to spare. My father and Bill Koikos would take people to the back booths, which were draped for privacy, and feed them right there so the customer didn't display the fact that he had no money to pay for his meal. Not only did they serve people doughnuts; they served vegetables, soup, or whatever else they had to spare from the steam table. The people in Bessemer never forgot that. The Bright Star became part of the family and remains so today. This was a period of people helping people to survive. This act of compassion further endeared the Bright Star to the citizens of Bessemer.

James O. Cain, a centenarian who was born at about the time the Bright Star was founded, also described the difficult economic times of the 1930s. "Man, that was a rough time here then," Cain recalled. "People weren't making no money, maybe three or four dollars a week. I ran a barber shop and we charged thirty-five cents for a haircut. When we went up a nickel or a dime, people threatened to quit us. People didn't have no money so we sometimes credited them month to month. One guy moved to Fairfield and left here owing us about fifty dollars. That was a lot of money. I used to cut Mr. Bill's hair and his brother, Pete's, too."

Willie Mae Phillips turned one hundred years old on October 28, 2006. She recalled trips to the Bright Star after visiting her husband, who was injured while working at Raymond Ore Mines, in Bessemer General Hospital. "I would walk up to the Bright Star the days I sat with him," she wrote to the Bright Star. "You made English pea soup that was the best tasting I ever ate. I was pregnant with my fourth son. It was the depression days and not much money in. Can't remember the price but know it wasn't very much. Only knew it was good."

The restaurant owned by "Post Office John" Bonduris was a casualty of the Great Depression. The business failed, leaving John virtually penniless. For the next nineteen years of his life, he managed the Realty Pool Room, which was located in the basement of the Bright Star until it was moved next door to a street-level site. The poolroom proved a popular gathering spot, not only for its recreational character but also because of the teletype machine located there. Baseball fans learned that they could get up-to-the-minute scores from their favorite teams while relaxing over a game of pool.

A Place in the Heart

The depression years served as the backdrop for an insightful look at the character of Constantine "Gus" Sarris, one of the Bright Star's owners at the time and the partner who was in charge of the kitchen. John D. Bonduris, Jr., provided the story:

> Gus Sarris was known to many as "Charlie Chaplin." His hair and his little mustache were a bit like Charlie Chaplin's and he sometimes came to a dance dressed like that. He loved children. His hard work and his long hours in the Bright Star's kitchen contributed immeasurably to its success and its place among the finest restaurants in the state of Alabama.
>
> Gus Sarris was a very loving individual, very kind, very hospitable, and he could not do enough for people that he really liked. I happened to be fortunate enough to have known him and to have received his love and his help. My mother, Gladys, knew Gus Sarris very well and, according to Gus, she was very kind to him. My mother died in 1935. It hurt Gus very badly, and the day of her funeral he came to the house and wanted to talk to me. Of course, a seven-year-old kid doesn't really know what is going on. He does but he doesn't. He doesn't understand what is really happening to him but Gus came to me and said, "I want to talk to you. Let's go in the back bedroom where we can talk."

> He said, "I feel so badly about your mother's death. She was so nice to me. There is one thing I want you to understand. Yes, you have lost a mother, but you have also gained a second father. If at any time you ever want anything, just come to me and we will be sure you get what you want."

Gus Sarris proved to be a man of his word. While walking with him one afternoon in downtown Bessemer, young John stopped in front of a hardware store to admire a wagon that was displayed in the window. "I really fell in love with it," Bonduris said. "It was unusual in the fact that the tires were inflatable. After seeing that wagon, we went to the Bright Star for one of Uncle Gus's famous doughnuts. I forgot about the wagon until I woke up on Christmas morning and found it under our tree. Santa Claus, in

Bill Koikos and Gus Sarris, ca. 1924. (Courtesy of the Koikos family.)

the form of Gus Sarris, had delivered it. The same proved true for a bicycle that Gus and I saw while we were visiting Long-Lewis Hardware. He told me to go over there and try it out. I loved it and, sure enough, it showed up under my Christmas tree the next year, courtesy of Gus Sarris."

Gus Sarris's generosity again manifested itself when Bonduris graduated from Phillips High School in Birmingham.

"I took the streetcar to Bessemer to have lunch with Uncle Gus," he related.

> He asked me to go with him to a local jewelry store as he was in need of a new watch. We went to the store, which was a few doors down from the Bright Star, and he asked me to help him pick out a watch. I pointed to several that I thought were very nice. One was a Longine Wittnauer, and it cost eighty-five dollars. He liked it, too, and said he would wait to buy it at another time. We got in his car to drive to Birmingham, but Uncle Gus said he forgot something in the store and would be right back. On our drive to Birmingham, he handed me a small box he pulled from a bag. "By the way," he said, "I got you something for your graduation." I opened the box and there was the watch. I still wear the watch from time to time and think of him and what a wonderful man he was.

Sarris's generosity was paralleled by his skill in the Bright Star's kitchen during the dark days of the depression. Always fond of wearing his white chef's hat, he

Bright Star's Greek-Style Snapper

This dish features the classic Greek combination of olive oil, lemon juice, and oregano.

juice of 3 lemons
oregano to taste
salt and pepper to taste
1 cup plus 2 tablespoons and 1 teaspoon extra-virgin olive oil
1 stick butter, melted
6 8-oz. fresh snapper fillets
1/2 cup flour, for dusting

Make sauce by mixing lemon juice, oregano, salt, and pepper in bowl with wire whisk. Slowly pour 1 cup plus 2 tablespoons olive oil into lemon mixture, whisking constantly until emulsified.

To prepare fish, brush melted butter over each fillet, coating evenly. Lightly dust each piece with flour. Cook in a heavy skillet coated with 1 teaspoon olive oil or on a griddle over medium heat until lightly browned and cooked through.

Pour sauce over broiled fish and serve immediately.

Serves 6.

could usually be found in the kitchen preparing his famous Greek snapper, which became a Bright Star signature dish.

Equally famous was his technique for filleting the fish, which is still used today at the Bright Star. Witnesses say that he began by holding the fish by the tail and running the knife the length of the fish, carefully removing the bone and skin. The boneless fillet was then prepared using Sarris's special seasonings.

Since times were lean, nothing was thrown away. Sarris would batter and fry the bones so that the meat nearest the bone could be eaten as well.

Sarris's own sweet tooth helped provide for those customers who craved a dessert to top off their meal. While pies had been on the menu for most of the restaurant's history, Sarris himself prepared the Bright Star's custard pies. "They were delicious, along with his famous doughnuts," John D. Bonduris, Jr., noted. "We don't know where the recipes came from or whether he learned to make those things here or while he was in Greece."

The hard times of the day also required resourcefulness in preparing the restaurant's menus. John D. Bonduris, Jr., pointed out that his father, John D. Bonduris, one of the Bright Star's owners at the time, oversaw much of that job. "My father was more or less a manager," Bonduris said. "He ensured that the help was there and the menus were made. They had to make their own menus with a machine that had a type of gelatin on it. My father would use his two fingers in a 'hunt and peck' system to type the letters that formed the menu. Then he would impact this page with the gelatin, put it on a little machine with a barrel that you turned, and reproduce the menu. He became fast and very good at it. He had to be. Getting that menu out for lunch was very important. People started coming in for lunch at around eleven o'clock and the menu had to be ready."

Bonduris recalled other characteristics about his father and his uncle Tom Bonduris, the restaurant's founder.

> Dad was a very kind, gentle person. He worked with the employees. He didn't have too much to say; he wasn't a big talker. You had to kind of push things out of him.
>
> Uncle Tom was a very fine man, too. He was very refined. Like my father, he was rather quiet, but he was very smart. Though he didn't have much formal education, he was smart in his own business way. He knew how to make money. He later invested in the stock market and made enough money to visit his sons Angelo in Chicago and Jimmy in San Antonio. I would characterize him as an old-style, aristocratic European. And his wife, Angeliki, was just a beautiful, elegant lady. It was easy to understand how he fell in love with her when he first saw her.

The one thing that really impressed me was how my father and Uncle Tom learned English the hard way by listening to people. It is very difficult because of the pronunciation of certain words. I was very privileged to have known Uncle Tom and Uncle Gus Sarris.

Cheerfulness Breaks Through

Despite the hard economic times, the people of Bessemer continued to celebrate holidays and special events at the Bright Star. The city itself also contributed to efforts to lift the spirits of its citizens during the holidays. Throughout the 1930s, an annual Christmas parade wound its way through downtown Bessemer. People lined the streets to wave at participants ranging from the mayor and city council to Santa Claus as they rode by. John D. Bonduris, Jr., remembered that "everybody came out to see the parade and then to shop. The merchants benefited greatly. The Lion's Club had an annual Lion's Pure Food Show where they displayed different items of food and one thing or another that people would buy to help the Lion's Club in its benefit drive.

"The scenery was what I remember most. All the merchants up and down the main street had their stores beautifully decorated, and even the light fixtures were decorated. Downtown Bessemer at that time was really beautiful."

Bill and Tasia

Halfway through the 1930s, Bill Koikos's life changed forever. One Sunday morning, while attending services at the Greek Orthodox Church in Birmingham, he noticed a tall, slender, dark-haired woman singing in the church choir.

Anastasia Microyiannakis had come to America in 1928 with her uncle George and aunt Eugenia Koutroulakis, who were on their honeymoon. She joined her father, Nicholas, who had come to America a few years before. A butcher by trade, Nicholas Microyiannikis worked at a restaurant called the Belmont Café in Birmingham.

Anastasia and her aunt and uncle had left their village of Sykea in the Peloponnesus region of Greece from which Bill Koikos had emigrated in 1920. Her father and mother had intended to bring other family members to Birmingham, but the hard times of the depression had put their plans on hold. Anastasia lived with Uncle George and Aunt Eugenia on Twenty-Sixth Street in Bessemer and helped with the couple's children, Gus, Tasia, and Sam, who were born in Birmingham. "My dad sent for me when I was twelve and a half years old," Anastasia (Tasia) recalled in a 1984 interview in the *Western Star.* "I came in 1928 to go to school. I lived in Norwood across from Norwood Hospital."

Having been introduced at church, Bill and Tasia came to know each other gradually under the strict chaperonage of her father. Tasia was barely twenty, and the prospect of marriage to Bill, with his kind, gentle personality and the stability provided by his ownership in the Bright Star, was an excellent one for her. Careful to follow the strict courtship protocol of the day, Bill informed his good friends Nicholas and Calliope Mitchinikos (later Mitchell) of his intention to ask Anastasia to marry him. They, in turn,

Anastasia Microyiannakis, age sixteen, neighbor Lula Melonas, and Gus Koutroulakis at the Koutroulakis home in Norwood, 1931. (Courtesy of the Koikos family.)

Engagement photograph of Anastasia Microyiannakis and Bill Koikos, 1935. (Courtesy of the Koikos family.)

would host a dinner at which the intended bride's family would meet the proposed suitor. Mr. and Mrs. Mitchinikos would then vouch for the young man's character. Chris Mitchell, the son of Mr. and Mrs. Mitchinikos, recalled,

> I was about eleven years old when Mr. Bill came to our house for dinner. We lived at the time at 705 Fourth Avenue West near Birmingham-Southern College. After dinner, I remember we all went into the living room of my parents' house. Mr. Bill stood up and announced to Mr. Microyiannakis that he wanted his daughter's hand in marriage. My father then stood up and vouched for Mr. Bill's character, his hard work, and his ability to provide a suitable home and future for the couple. Tasia's father gave his permission and offered his blessings to the union. My father poured everyone a glass of wine to toast the engagement. It was quite an evening.

Tasia later recalled the event in the interview in the *Western Star:* "We had an engagement party and we married in the Holy Trinity Greek Orthodox Church in Birmingham, the old one, very small." When asked if she had had other boyfriends, she smiled. "No, no others," she replied.

Bill and Tasia were married on a snowy Thursday, January 23, 1936, at the Greek Orthodox Church in Birmingham. Even though the difference in their ages (Anastasia was born in 1915 and Bill was born in 1894) was considerable, it was not uncommon during those days for such a marriage to take place. Immigrant couples were often twenty or more years apart in age.

After a honeymoon trip to Biloxi, Mississippi, the couple lived for six months at the Gary Hotel, which was located on Second Avenue between Eighteenth and Nineteenth streets in Bessemer. The site is the present location of the city jail. Gus Sarris, Bill's partner in the Bright Star, lived at the same hotel.

Georgia Louzis Dikis, a lifelong friend of the Koikos family, remembers the deep friendship between her parents and Bill and Tasia Koikos.

> In 1928, my mother [Christine Catechis Louzis], age twelve, left the island of Corfu, Greece, with her parents. She met another twelve-year-old girl, Anastasia Microyiannakis. On the ship they became fast friends when they realized they were heading to the same place—Birmingham, Alabama.
>
> Christine and Tasia had much in common. Christine was a bridesmaid in Tasia and Bill's wedding. They each married in 1936 and had three children.
>
> Tasia and Bill Koikos and Christine and George Louzis took trips to Tarpon Springs for the Feast

Day of Epiphany on January 6 and had many amusing adventures. My mother would also meet "Thea" Tasia at Joy Young's, a restaurant in Birmingham, for lunch and a whiskey sour. They had such fun and always were like young girls when they were together. They enjoyed being members of "Knit-Chat-Chew" [social club] along with other friends of their era and had lunch at each other's houses.

Bill finally moved his bride into their new home at 1428 Dartmouth Avenue, where they would spend the rest of their lives together. Tasia's father lived with them until he returned to Greece in 1946. Bill and Tasia's first child, Helen, was born on May 5, 1937.

Helen and Jimmy Koikos, ages five and four, 1942. (Courtesy of the Koikos family.)

Nicky Koikos, ten months old, 1946. (Courtesy of the Koikos family.)

"I was named after my father's mother," Helen noted.

My brother Jimmy [Demetrios] was named for my father's father. He came along on April 21 of the following year. He was about two months premature and weighed about three and a half pounds, so it was something of a miracle that he survived. My mother promised God that if He spared Jimmy's life, she would never spank him. If Mama had known what a mischievous child she'd just had, she wouldn't have made that promise!

I think my parents thought they were through having children until Nicholas (named after his maternal grandfather) came along seven years later on August 16, 1945. My dad was feeling pretty proud since he was in his early fifties at the time. I remember that just two days before Nicky was born, the Japanese had surrendered to end World War II and there was a great celebration.

Helen recalled her early childhood on Dartmouth Avenue for the *Western Star.*

When my brothers and I were little, we pretty much stayed at home with our mother. It was not until we were about ten or twelve years old that we started going to the restaurant. It was a real treat for us to go the Bright Star. I remember the kindness and friendliness of "Uncle" Gus Sarris when he greeted us there.

Mama felt it was her duty at the time to take care of us at home and keep Daddy healthy and happy at the restaurant. After all, he was the one who was providing a living for our family.

It was great growing up in Bessemer. We had a parkway in the middle of the street with rose bushes on each end, and in the center we played Red Rover and Simon Says. We had a square dance club in the garage and everyone paid dues of twenty-five cents.

I remember there was a commissary in the area where the people who worked at the Muscoda mines shopped. Many of them lived in company housing near the mines. Their children went to Arlington School, as I did, and we made friends. We played as kids together near the railroad track that ran to Fairfield. It was a wonderful community.

The families we grew up with were Sam and Lily Boackle and their eight children, the Wallace Veasey family, the Rose Atchison family, the John Rockett family, and the Giles Hathaway family.

Glimmers of Hope

The Great Depression would linger through most of the 1930s, but the faint rumblings of economic activity were finally being heard by the end of the decade. President Roosevelt's New Deal policies had introduced a number of major changes in the structure of the American economy through increased government regulation and massive public works projects designed to promote recovery. Still, by 1939 about 15 percent of the workforce remained unemployed.

The slight improvement in the national economy eventually trickled down to Bessemer. The Pullman plant had come back to life in 1934 when Seaboard Lines placed an order for 900 cars. During the next two years, more than 1,500 railroad cars were produced. The city received a major boost in 1937 when 5,859 railroad cars were assembled and shipped from the Bessemer facility. The plant proved to be a major factor in Bessemer's economy, ultimately employing approximately 1,800 men. Pullman was the youngest railroad-car-building plant in the South and became one of the most efficient and largest producers of freight cars and parts in the country.

In 1935, the new U.S. Highway 11 connecting Bessemer to Birmingham was built. The following year, Bessemer dedicated the first high school football stadium in Alabama to have lights for nighttime play. In 1937 the city and the chamber of commerce celebrated Bessemer's fiftieth anniversary, and the following year saw the opening of the Dixie Metal Company. "The programs of President Roosevelt finally began taking effect in the Birmingham/Bessemer area," stated Nicky Koikos. "It took World War II, however, to really get Bessemer's economy growing. To this day, a small oval picture of President Roosevelt hangs in the front area of the restaurant."

Clouds on the Horizon

The world continued to stretch its legs after the long economic sleep of the 1930s as men went back to work. There was growing concern, however, over the ominous storm clouds that were again hovering over Europe and Asia. Germany had rearmed after World War I and the Nazis had come to power. Japan had invaded China in 1937 and sacked its capital, Nanking, while slaughtering more than 360,000 Chinese civilians and prisoners of war.

When Hitler's troops invaded Poland in 1939, those clouds burst. Britain and France declared war on Germany on September 3. Two years later, the U.S. Pacific fleet at Pearl Harbor was attacked without warning on a Sunday morning by Japanese planes winging in from distant aircraft carriers. America became part of the struggle, and Bessemer's industries went on a wartime footing.

This time, however, the manufacturing operations took on a different look. As most able-bodied men enlisted or were drafted into military service, women began replacing them on assembly lines in Bessemer and across the country.

In 1942, the Pullman plant received government contracts to build railroad freight cars for overseas army use. Thousands of tons of steel from Jefferson County's foundries were needed to meet production of everything from railcars and trucks to bomb casings. By 1943, the Pullman plant was turning out eighteen newly designed composite hopper cars per day and fifty army boxcars. In addition, the plant was producing fifty caboose cars per day.

Unemployment throughout America dropped rapidly as U.S. factories, including the manufacturing operations in Bessemer and Birmingham, were flooded with orders for arms and munitions.

The Bright Star during the War Years

"During the years of World War II, the main thing you would see in Bessemer were the stars in the windows of homes that had a family member in the military," recalled John D. Bonduris, Jr. "We had air raid wardens near the Koikos home. My dad was an air raid warden and wore a white steel helmet and carried a flashlight. It was his job to go around and make sure that everybody had their lights off during an air raid warning. The siren would go off at city hall, which meant an air raid warning was underway. During the warning, people would turn off their lights and downtown became black."

The Bright Star welcomed a variety of customers during the war years. Businesspeople, shoppers, and storeowners in the downtown area would come in during the morning and afternoon, but the evenings were popular with families.

"We had a record player in the front of the restaurant and Bing Crosby was particularly popular during that time," noted John D. Bonduris, Jr.

> That type of music provided a nice atmosphere for people who were having dinner. We also had a jukebox there and people often played their own selections.
>
> Of particular interest was the radio we had sitting right on the counter where many people ate. It was a strange size—about three feet long and about five or six inches deep with a speaker on top. With all the war news being broadcast, that radio got a lot of use. People enjoyed listening to it. They would sit at the counter and eat their meals or drink their coffee and listen to the news. I don't know what happened to it but it was something that people really enjoyed.

The Bright Star's workforce, like that in industries across the nation, underwent a sea change. "The transition from male to female servers began in the 1940s with the new role of women in the workplace during the war years," recalled Nicky Koikos. "Prior to that, servers were traditionally male. My daddy,

Large party at the Bright Star, 1942. (Courtesy of the Koikos family.)

Gus Sarris, and Tom Bonduris had all been waiters. After the war, more women began working as servers."

One notable example of a woman who made a difference in the Bright Star, even before World War II, was Irene Pickens. Pickens and her husband came to Bessemer from the Midwest in 1937. Upon entering the Bright Star one day for lunch she struck up a conversation with then owner John Bonduris. When he heard that she was new in town and seeking employment, Bonduris quickly offered the sophis-

The Bright Star, 1938. Bill Koikos and John D. Bonduris are behind the counter. Note the ornate cash register sitting on the end of the counter, and the radio behind it against the mirror. (Courtesy of the Koikos family.)

ticated and attractive brunette a job as a waitress. She accepted and was employed at the Bright Star for nineteen years. As well as serving as both a waitress and a cashier, Pickens undertook managerial duties, which was unusual for a woman at that time. Her work at the Bright Star paved the way for women such as Myrtle Williams, Carrie Lee LeFurgey, Brenda Salser, and Sonya Twitty to work at all levels of the restaurant's operations.

A look at the Bright Star's menu during the 1940s reveals some interesting changes. In 1940, a vegetable dinner with dessert and a drink went for forty cents. Roast turkey with dressing was one dollar. Pork chops were sixty cents. A shrimp cocktail cost thirty-five cents. Eighty-five cents bought a half chicken, and a porterhouse steak went for $1.50.

Jo Ann Barr of Bessemer shared a memory of eating at the Bright Star during her childhood in the 1940s. "My mother and father took me as a small child to the Bright Star," she recalled. "My favorite things to eat then were the tenderloin of trout (that was what it was called back then—not trout almondine) and the steak served on a sizzling platter. You could hear the waitress approaching your table with the steak sizzling and popping on the metal platter. Back then there was always olive oil and vinegar served in cruets on each table—no fancy salad dressings."

Proof that the Bright Star had a strong foothold both economically and emotionally in the heart of Bessemer comes from the following story, related by Bill Koikos's son Jimmy.

> In the 1940s, the Haggerty brothers [then owners of the Realty Building, where the Bright Star was located] came to the four Bright Star partners and told them that when the present lease expired, they would have to move. As owners of the building, they were negotiating with a chain restaurant out of New York to move in there. Jap Bryant was mayor of Bessemer at the time. A number of local businesspeople came to him and told him that the Bright Star could not move. They pleaded with him to persuade the Haggerty brothers to renegotiate the lease with the Bright Star's partners. Mayor Bryant prevailed, and the Bright Star did not have to close.

Janet Humphries shared this story of a special visit to the Bright Star during her childhood.

> My memory of the Bright Star started in 1947, the year my father got killed in a truck wreck. . . . Mother, who is now ninety years old, brought us four children back to Bessemer where our families lived. One Saturday in the summer of 1947 Mother put us on the bus and we went to the Grand Theatre in Bessemer. As we were leaving we told Mother we were hungry. We were walking down Nineteenth Street so Mother took all four of us into the Bright Star to eat. Mother ordered us all a hotdog and drink. . . . Mother asked the man who waited on our table for the bill. The nice man told her the lunch was paid. He went on to say that we were nice children. That she did not owe anything. . . .
>
> This has been on my mind over the years. This is what the Bright Star means to my family and me. . . . This is the fondest memory of my life.

Another customer, Lorene Adkins, contributed a story about her husband, herself, and the Bright Star.

We met in a Walgreen's next door to the Bright Star—1943—all the kids went there to hang out. The war was on and we had to do all we wanted to do fast! He was going to go in the air force. We married six weeks later, January 1944.

For our forty-fifth anniversary he took me back where we met. It was a jewelry store then and he bought me earrings. Then he took me to the Bright Star to eat. The jewelry store is now part of the Bright Star. . . .

This is how we met and the Bright Star was always the special place for us until I lost him in 1990. This helps me go back in time.

Greek Dressing

Oil and vinegar cruets are still available at the Bright Star, but this Greek dressing is more popular. Customers eat it on house salads as well as on Greek salads.

1/3 cup red wine vinegar
1/4 cup lemon juice
1/2 tablespoon lemon-pepper seasoning
1/4 teaspoon salt
1/4 teaspoon Greek seasoning
1/2 teaspoon chopped fresh garlic
1 teaspoon dried oregano
1/4 cucumber, sliced and seeded
1/4 cup feta cheese, crumbled
1/2 cup extra-virgin olive oil
1 cup light olive or other vegetable oil

Combine all ingredients EXCEPT OILS in blender. With blender running, slowly add olive oil and vegetable oil through center opening in blender lid to emulsify.

Makes 2 cups.

Toward the end of the war, it became evident that the Bright Star would survive the difficult war days just as it had weathered the economic hard times of the 1930s. It was also becoming evident, however, that the business would be hard-pressed to continue to support the families of four partners. In 1944, John D. Bonduris, one of the second generation of owners, sold his interest to the three remaining partners and moved to Birmingham, where he had an opportunity to join the owners of Jeb's Seafood Restaurant. Bill Koikos and his brother Pete, along with Gus Sarris, would continue to operate the Bright Star.

Postwar Recovery

Hostilities in World War II finally came to a close with Germany's unconditional surrender to the Allies on May 5, 1945, and the Japanese capitulation four months later. America's industries, which had gone to war with high-speed emergency production, just as spiritedly led the way to converting their facilities to peacetime operations.

Bessemer's manufacturing plants followed suit. By late 1947, Pullman employees were producing 1,000 railroad cars a month. The following year, the plant set three production records, one of which was for shipping more than 11,000 domestic railcars in a single year.

The city itself boasted numerous infrastructure improvements. A new park was named after city founder Henry F. Debardeleben, and the Mary Susan Bryant Bridge was completed on Ninth Avenue. The Bessemer Electric and Water Company was created to serve 11,000 customers.

The lights had come on again and the magic was back in Bessemer. The three remaining partners at the Bright Star had steered their business through the lean times of the Great Depression and World War II. The restaurant had survived while many other businesses had failed by adhering to the principles of its founders—to provide quality food and good service at reasonable prices. Along the way, Bill Koikos, Pete Koikos, Gus Sarris, and John D. Bonduris had become known for providing something else. They had offered a helping hand when times were hard to people who had little reason to smile. In doing so, their restaurant had become more than a place to eat. The Bright Star was now a part of the social fabric of the community.

Bill Koikos outside the Bright Star Café, 1939. (Courtesy of the Koikos family.)

★4★

In Its Prime

The 1950s

My dad taught me how to work and how to save money.
—Jimmy Koikos

Economic Ups and Downs

The post–World War II years proved to be exciting times of change for Bessemer, the South, and America in general. Industries and manufacturing operations had returned to a peacetime footing after the war ended, and the surge in economic activity was soon noticed in Bessemer as new businesses cropped up in western Jefferson County. The completion of the Bessemer Super Highway, an expansion of Ninth Avenue, made it a short, easy drive to neighboring Birmingham, and the highway connecting Bessemer to Tuscaloosa was improved. In 1955, a Holiday Inn motel, only the fifth in that newly founded lodging chain, opened on the Bessemer Super Highway.

The face of the city itself was changing. The year 1950 saw the removal of streetcars and tracks from the downtown area. The board of education added a new junior high school to the city's school system in 1952. Two years later, the city's residents turned out to celebrate Bessemer High School's victory in the state football championships.

Jess E. Lanier was elected mayor of Bessemer in 1956, and would serve in that capacity for eighteen years. Under his leadership, the city made significant strides in expanding its economic base and attracting new business.

The city's progress was very timely, as disturbing economic trends followed closely on the heels of this postwar prosperity. Many of the area's ore mines began closing in the 1950s and early 1960s, as ore from

Venezuela began replacing the locally mined product. Steel from Scandinavia also began making huge inroads into the U.S. market.

The pinch was felt in Bessemer, Birmingham, and other industrial centers. Soon, Woodward Iron, Republic Steel, Sloss Furnaces, Jefferson County's many coal and ore mines, and other major employers in the area became mere shadows of their former selves and eventually closed.

The 1950s at the Star

Meanwhile the Bright Star, in its fifth decade, had long since become a Bessemer institution. Under the guidance of Bill and Pete Koikos and Gus Sarris, the restaurant continued to serve breakfast, lunch, and dinner nearly every day of the year. Breakfast regulars could be folks popping in for a quick meal before work, or clublike gatherings lingering over coffee and doughnuts. Lunch brought businessmen discussing trade and downtown shoppers. Families often came to the Bright Star for dinner, and large parties, whether business related or for private special occasions, made use of the Bright Star's famous back booths.

The installation of central air conditioning in 1952 demonstrated the ongoing efforts of the Bright Star's owners to provide their customers with the best in service and amenities. In addition to enjoying the restaurant's fine food, customers would come to the Bright Star to escape the oppressive heat of an Alabama summer. The skylight that had allowed for air circulation was covered. The restaurant's fans were removed, and one was relocated to the front porch of the Koikos family home on Dartmouth Avenue. The improvements were heralded by the staff as well as by the Bright Star's customers. The waitresses in particular were overjoyed by the cooler working conditions.

The kitchen staff, however, continued to experience the heat of their workspace. An advanced exhaust system had been installed in the late 1940s, but it did little to dispel the cooking heat. Longtime employee Walter Hoskins said about those pre–air conditioning days, "When you finished a shift you were soaking wet from head to foot. When you took your clothes off you had salt in your shoes and clothes." Air conditioning would not make its appearance in the Bright Star kitchen until 1975. Even then, it was one of the first in the Birmingham area.

Nicky Koikos recounted the day-to-day functioning of the restaurant in the 1950s.

> Our breakfast business at that time was not large, since we didn't open until eight o'clock. However, every morning at about nine, people began gradually filling the Bright Star's seats to sip coffee and exchange news.
>
> Lunch at the Bright Star in the 1950s was primarily of the meat-and-three variety. The meats were

usually chicken or beef and we had a variety of vegetables, including potatoes, beans, squash, and okra.

In those days, all lunch and dinner orders were turned in orally through the windows into the kitchen. The waitresses did a tremendous job because they had to remember all their orders. The waitresses at other restaurants, like John's in downtown Birmingham, did the same thing. It was not until the early 1960s that the waitresses at the Bright Star began writing down their orders.

Two members of the kitchen staff who particularly assisted Gus Sarris with the lunch vegetables and with dinner in those days were Sweet Love Church and Miss Nathan. Miss Nathan, I remember, prepared the broiled entrees beautifully.

Cousin Jimmy N. Koikos of Tallahassee, Florida, is the oldest son of Bill Koikos's brother Nick. The old "Peleta Pipeline," though unused for thirty or so years, came into play again with the arrival of sixteen-year-old Jimmy N. to Bessemer in 1951. He worked as a waiter until 1958, and he recalled this era at the Bright Star in a 2006 interview.

Uncle Bill always smiled and appreciated the guests. He dressed impeccably—his shoes shined, shirt perfect, always said "yes ma'am" and "no ma'am" to guests. He demanded that his employees extend the same courtesy to the guests at the restaurant.

Gus Sarris stayed in the kitchen and was extremely hardworking. He never married and lived at the Gary Hotel his whole life. He would come in and work breakfast and lunch, leave for two hours, and close every night. He had every other Sunday off.

Cornbread Muffins

No meat and three at the Bright Star would be complete without a basket of these traditional Southern favorites, which are made from this twenty-five-year-old recipe.

1 pound self-rising cornmeal
1/2 cup self-rising flour
2 tablespoons sugar
2 eggs, well beaten
1 cup whole milk
1/2 cup buttermilk
3 tablespoons butter, melted

Preheat oven to 375°. Grease mini-muffin pans (preferably cast iron) with cooking spray. Place pans in oven to heat up. Combine cornmeal, flour, and sugar, and set aside. In a separate bowl, add eggs to whole milk and buttermilk and beat well. Add butter and beat well. Fold egg mixture into dry ingredients. Blend quickly and pour batter into hot muffin pans. Bake 15 minutes until golden brown.

Makes 24 muffins.

> The kitchen was small. At that time, the cooks did all the prep work themselves. For example, whole sides of pork were brought in, and the cooks cut the steaks themselves. Whole carrots and other vegetables were brought in—nothing was precut or canned. Everything was cheaper back then.
>
> I remember in the 1950s the popularity of the private back booths. There were six couples who ate there every Saturday night.

Mary McCarroll Sherrod worked at the Bright Star from 1949 until 1997, and she added these memories about working in the back of the restaurant in the 1950s.

> I started out washing dishes. I moved on later to cooking. It was hot in the kitchen. Didn't have air conditioning then. The renovation [of 1966] made a lot of improvements.
>
> Gus Sarris was in the kitchen in those days. I was kind of afraid of him, but he was a good man. I remember we had snapper throats on the menu in those days, too. We also had many of the items on the menu today, like the red snapper and other fish. My salary when I started was $12 a week. Other people in the kitchen back then were Earnestine, Fannie, and Glenn.
>
> Mr. Bill and Miss Tasia were my favorites. I loved them, and I love Jimmy and Nicky, too. Jimmy said I cared more about Nicky than about him, but I guess it's because he was the baby.
>
> I enjoyed the years I worked at the Bright Star. I was kind of like a mother to the kitchen staff.

A major factor in the increasing success of the Bright Star was the quality and loyalty of the waitresses and the kitchen staff. Nicky Koikos stated,

> My father always felt that the high quality of the employees was crucial to the image he wanted to portray of the Bright Star. Our servers were known to our customers as people who really enjoyed their jobs. They had a wonderful relationship with our family.
>
> One of the reasons the servers and the kitchen staff enjoyed their jobs is the fact that they knew the family respected them. That was very important. They always referred to the management as "Mr. Bill," "Mr. Pete," and "Mr. Gus." And my daddy and Uncle Pete and Uncle Gus always referred to the servers as "Miss Thelma" or "Miss Sherry."
>
> Our servers felt a great loyalty to the Bright Star and they were proud to be working there. The success of the Bright Star is due in large part to those people.

Helen Koikos as a Bessemer High School cheerleader, 1954. (Courtesy of the Cocoris family.)

A Family Grows Up

The Koikos home on Dartmouth Avenue was also experiencing change during these years. Helen and Jimmy had attended Arlington School on Arlington Avenue and entered Bessemer High School in the early 1950s. Nicky, the "surprise baby," would follow a few years later.

A highlight of Helen's teenage years was a trip to Peleta with her father in 1952. Bill Koikos recalled the visit in a 1984 interview that ran in the *Western Star*. "I went back with Helen in 1952 and stayed three months," he said. "I didn't like it because I tried to compare it to Bessemer. There were not many conveniences in my village—no indoor plumbing or running water, no electricity or telephone—and I was glad to get back home."

Tasia also made a trip to Greece in the early 1960s. "Helen took me in 1962 to visit my mother in Sykea and my 104-year-old mother-in-law in Peleta," she recalled in that same interview. "Everything was different there. I was also glad to get back home."

Helen graduated from Bessemer High School in 1955. She had a job at the Bright Star during her

Left:
Bill Koikos with his mother, Eleni, in Peleta, Greece, 1952. (Courtesy of the Koikos family.)

Below:
Helen (front row, center) and Bill (back row, second from right) Koikos with relatives in Peleta, Greece, 1952. Tassos N. Koikos and George N. Koikos, Helen's first cousins, are in the back row, left. In the background, another cousin, Panos N. Koikos, sits on a stone wall. (Courtesy of the Koikos family.)

high school years writing the checks that went out to food vendors every week. Helen enrolled at Birmingham Southern College in 1955; she graduated with a degree in elementary education four years later. On Friday nights she would come home to act as hostess at the Bright Star. After graduation, her first assignment was as a third-grade teacher at N. H. Price, an elementary school in the Birmingham system.

The Boys Try Their Hand

During their early childhood, the Koikos siblings visited the restaurant relatively rarely and then only to eat. Inevitably, however, Bill's two sons began to work at the Bright Star, both to test whether restaurant work was their calling and because their help was genuinely needed. Jimmy Koikos recalled working at the Bright Star as a fourteen-year-old.

> I came to work at the Bright Star in 1952. My sister, Helen, had just gone with my dad to Greece. I'd get there in the morning and sweep the floor. Then I'd mop it with a mop that was bigger than I was. Afterward, we would sprinkle a bit of sawdust on the floor. I also worked as a busboy clearing dishes off the tables. I picked up dishes and glasses in a bus pan that is still at the Bright Star today.
>
> I worked there in the summer months, on weekends, and after school. The Bright Star is the only place I've ever worked.
>
> I was paid $10 per week. They took out twenty-five cents for Social Security, leaving me with $9.75. I was allowed to keep $4.75, but my dad made me put the remaining five dollars in an account I had at the First Federal Bank next door to the Bright Star. I still have that bankbook showing my deposits. Sometimes I wanted to keep the entire $9.75, but my dad was insistent.
>
> "No! Next door!" he would shout. My dad taught me how to work and how to save money.

Nicky Koikos was a youngster during the 1950s and recalled his time at the Bright Star during those years.

> I remember Jimmy and my dad going to the restaurant early in the morning during the summer months to scrub the beautiful octagon tile. When it was cleaned the green and burgundy shone against the white background. The floor virtually gleamed with a "hospital" type of clean.
>
> Some of my earliest memories of the Bright Star are of going there with my daddy when he opened up the restaurant in the mornings. I was about ten years old in 1955 when I began going with him to help out. I never scrubbed the floors like Jimmy did. My first job was to prepare the iced tea. I would

put ice in the tea glasses and make them available for the waitresses. We wanted them to be able to get them easily and take them quickly to the customers.

We had a long counter with seventeen stools at that time, and I was allowed to wait on a single customer on one stool. When I was about eleven years old, in 1956, one of our servers named Myrtle Williams taught me how to serve coffee. She told me not to look at it while I carried it, as that would tend to make it shake. She also taught me how to write orders using the correct abbreviations for different items.

I remember waiting often on a Mr. Isadore Rosen, a friend of the family who had a department store in town. He would talk to my daddy every day. Mr. Rosen wanted his food served quickly so he could return to work.

Customer Recollections

Through daily interaction with the citizens of Bessemer, front men Bill and Pete Koikos made lasting impressions on their customers. Paula Jenkins McPoland shared this childhood memory of Mr. Bill and the Bright Star:

Being born and raised in Bessemer, Alabama, there was only one nice restaurant to enjoy. That, of course, was the Bright Star. Yes, we had the Town Clock Cafeteria, McClellan's sandwich counter, the Post House, etc., but nothing could ever compare to visiting the Bright Star.

My first memories of this Bessemer treasure were when I was a little girl. Mr. Bill Koikos would always give me a cigar box to use at school to hold my pencils and crayons. After eating there, he would always treat me to an after-dinner mint. I know this isn't much today, but to a little girl it was something special. He was such a lovely, gentle man.

Another Bessemer native, Gloria Ann Campbell Parks, wrote about her encounter with Pete Koikos as a teenager.

In 1954, Sandy Thompson, David Farr, Royce Braden, "John-Boy" Rockett, and I were sharing two Cokes at the Bright Star when David dared me to stand up and start singing. I saw a table of Italian Americans and started singing "That's Amore." Immediately Mr. Koikos started heading my way, and

> everyone ran except me. Mr. Koikos didn't like any nonsense in his restaurant, but the Italian family started applauding. To my surprise, Mr. Koikos said, "You know Greek song?" I replied, "No, but I can learn." He told me to come back when I learned a Greek song and tell my friends to bring enough money for four Cokes, because mine would be on the house!

The 1950s were a period of calm prosperity for the Bright Star. Its three owners were in their prime and well established in their adopted homeland. No major changes in the running of the restaurant occurred over the course of the decade. The 1960s, however, would prove as full of new experiences for the venerable restaurant as that decade was for the country as a whole.

★5★

New Face of the South

The 1960s

More importantly, our family realized it was the right thing to do.
—Nicky Koikos

Changes for the Better

The overall prosperity of the postwar years lasted well into the 1960s. Bessemer Memorial Hospital opened with 127 beds in 1964. Two years later, Bessemer State Technical College began welcoming new students. The chamber of commerce launched a drive to secure funding for an airport for Bessemer. Ground was broken in 1968 on Westlake Mall, as the city followed this national phenomenon in shopping. A new high school named after Mayor Jess Lanier opened its doors to more than 1,300 Bessemer students.

In addition to the changes that were taking place in business and industry in the 1960s, major social changes were also underway that would affect the next decade profoundly. In its landmark *Brown v. Board of Education* decision of 1954, the U.S. Supreme Court ruled that racial segregation in the public schools was unconstitutional.

Birmingham had become the epicenter of the struggle for civil rights in 1963, and the eyes of the world focused on the Edmund Pettus Bridge in Selma, Alabama, when marchers en route to Montgomery were attacked by police and state troopers on March 9, 1965, which came to be known as "Bloody Sunday."

The winds of change continued blowing across the South with civil rights workers fighting the forces of bigotry in long and bitter campaigns to register African American voters who had long been disenfranchised through effective Jim Crow practices, such as literacy tests and poll taxes. In August 1965, President Johnson signed the Voting Rights Act, which prohibited the denial or abridgment of the right through literacy tests on a nationwide basis.

The guarantee of voting rights and the integration of the schools, parks, and other public places in Jefferson County and in the City of Bessemer finally became an accepted part of life in this area as it had been for years in other regions of the country. Restaurants in the area began admitting black patrons and expanding their hiring practices.

The Bright Star's owners took an impressive stance on the issue and exhibited an attitude far ahead of the conventional thinking of the time. Nicky Koikos recalled those years.

> My dad and Uncle Gus and Jimmy said they would serve all customers who came to the Bright Star, regardless of race. Gus was particularly vocal on the issue. He said that he had worked with black people for a long time and felt that certain wrongs needed to be righted. That was a bold, progressive statement, especially during those years.
>
> There was, naturally, some discussion about integration among our customers, but we felt we had a very loyal customer base. Everyone realized that equality among the races was the law of the land and the way things would be. More importantly, our family realized it was the right thing to do.

Jimmy added his memories of those years in an article titled "Greeks in Birmingham" published in 2004 by Southern Foodways Alliance. "Integration began taking place in this area around 1957 or 1958," he said. "It was about the time the armed forces were integrated. It took place here and there wasn't a second thought given to it."

Turning Sixty

The 1960s saw the Bright Star on the eve of its sixtieth birthday. The small café that Tom Bonduris had opened in a boomtown more than a half century before had changed greatly since 1907, and the new decade would bring yet another phase in its history.

Peter Koikos retired from the restaurant in 1960. Involved with the Bright Star since 1912, he was ready to pass the torch after almost fifty years in the business. He would remain in Bessemer until he died in 1977. His wife, Thalia, continued to live in their house on Second Avenue until her death in 1993.

Helen Koikos Cocoris recalled the contrasting management styles of her father and her uncle Pete.

There was always a lot of respect among Daddy, Uncle Pete, and Gus. My dad was younger than his brother Pete and would acquiesce to his wishes. Uncle Pete had been responsible for bringing my dad to America from Greece and helping him get started here. My daddy never forgot that, and always respected and honored Uncle Pete.

Daddy was the great middleman in the group. Uncle Pete's style was more severe and authoritative, while my dad was more passive. He was a perfect liaison between the servers and the kitchen staff and Uncle Pete. They both had a great relationship with our customers.

With the retirement of Peter Koikos, Bill brought his sons in as full partners over the course of the decade. Jimmy Koikos explained his increasing involvement with the Bright Star.

After my time at the university, my dad's brother Pete was fixing to retire. He asked me if I was coming here to work. I told him I'd come in and help out, but I didn't want to work in the restaurant business. He told me that in order to make any money, I needed to go into business for myself and not work for the other fellow. So I changed my mind and came to work full-time at the Bright Star on January 1, 1960.

We were open every day but Christmas, and we served breakfast, lunch, and dinner. We arrived every morning at seven a.m. About thirty years ago, I finally convinced my dad to discontinue offering breakfast.

Bessemer had undergone a lot of changes during the 1950s. The Holiday Inn had opened in 1953, and the restaurant there took a lot of the local business. Other restaurants were locating in the area as well. When I came to work at the Bright Star in 1960, I felt that we had to make a number of changes to successfully compete.

There was a woman who had been a waitress for eighteen years and was a fixture at the Bright Star. I found, however, that she was resistant to progress and to making any changes in the way we did business. She didn't want to revise the menu or anything else. I wasn't able to work with her, so one day I fired her. I remember my legs were shaking that day because I was so scared.

I felt it was time for a change in our menu with new specialty dishes and other items. I looked at the menus of other restaurants and I got a lot of ideas and suggestions. Back then, we offered seafood such as Greek snapper, which was filleted by Gus Sarris. He did an incredible job filleting the fish, and people would love to watch him work. The procedure he introduced for filleting fish is still followed today.

Greek snapper on the menu in those days was $2.95. Today it's $23.95.

Family gathering in a back booth at the Bright Star, 1964. This seems to have taken place soon after John and Helen Cocoris were married, since their wedding album is lying on the table. Seated, from left: Marguerite Sarris, John Cocoris, Jimmy Zamboukos, and Thalia Koikos. Standing, from left: Helen Koikos Cocoris, Chrisoula Zamboukos (Tasia Koikos's sister), Pete Koikos, Jimmy Koikos, Tasia Koikos, Mike Sarris, Anastasia Cocoris (John's mother), and Gus Cocoris (John's father).

Family gathering in a back booth at the Bright Star, 1961. Seated, from left: Jimmy Koikos, Bill Koikos, and Helen Koikos. Standing, from left: Gus Sarris, Nicky Koikos, and Tasia Koikos.

Members of the Koikos family in front of the Bright Star Café, 1964. From left: Jimmy N. Koikos (nephew of Bill Koikos), his wife, Ann Patronis Koikos, Bill Koikos, Jimmy Koikos, Pete Koikos, Helen Koikos Cocoris, Nicky Koikos, and Tasia Koikos.

Tartar Sauce

In Greece, fried fish is traditionally eaten with skordalia, a garlicky potato sauce. At the Bright Star, customers enjoy their fried snapper with this tartar sauce, which is made on-site every day. Cook Betty Bailey brought this recipe to the Bright Star from the Holiday Inn on the Bessemer Super Highway more than twenty-five years ago.

1 quart commercial-style salad dressing
2 10-ounce jars pickle relish
1/2 bell pepper, finely chopped
1/2 onion, finely chopped
1/3 carrot, finely chopped
1/2 teaspoon minced garlic
juice of 1/2 lemon

Mix all ingredients until well blended. Refrigerate until served.

Yields 1 quart.

Nicky, seven years younger than his brother, was still in high school when Jimmy began working full-time.

"I began working on making out the Bright Star's payroll while I was in high school from 1960 until 1963," said Nicky.

I remember sometimes bringing a date to the Bright Star for dinner. We would sit at one of the back booths and eat fried chicken.

We had four private booths at that time, and my daddy felt that those booths were the backbone of the Bright Star. A booth could seat eight people, and we could connect two of them together to seat a party of sixteen by removing the partitions between them. People went back there for privacy. They remain an important part of the Bright Star today.

Nicky told of the improvement in efficiency and productivity in the early 1960s kitchen that was attributable to four loyal and dependable female cooks: "Earnestine Barnes Smith, Fannie M. Wright, Mary McCarroll Sherrod, and Gwendolyn Joyce Atkinson. Under their influence, the old habit of calling orders in through the kitchen window was changed to a system of handwritten tickets that could be consulted by the cooks as they worked. This led to a much quieter, more professional kitchen capable of handling the increased volume of customers. With the handwritten-order system came the use of food runners to carry trays directly to the servers in the dining room, thus increasing the speed with which patrons could receive their food."

Meanwhile a major improvement in the professionalism of the waitstaff occurred with the hiring of Myrtle Williams. After four years as a server, she became head server in 1960. She immediately upgraded the appearance of the waitstaff, requiring crisp white uniforms, black satin aprons, and polished white shoes. Williams competed in the "Server of the Year" contest in Montgomery in 1962 and finished in second place, but at the Bright Star, she was second to none. Her leadership style was characterized by complete fairness and an ability to motivate her staff to meet the Bright Star's high service standards. She would never ask her employees to do anything that she would not do herself. She remained head server until 1972, when she began performing bookkeeping duties until her retirement in 1983.

Nicky Koikos had enrolled at the University of Alabama after he graduated from Bessemer High School. Upon graduation in 1968, he joined the National Guard. While he was stationed in South Carolina, his mother visited one weekend and told him that Gus Sarris was retiring from the business and

Bright Star servers Kay Ricci, Irene Higgs, Shelba Smith, and Myrtle Williams; owners Gus Sarris and Bill Koikos, October 1965. (Courtesy of the Koikos family.)

that there was a place for him at the Bright Star if that's what he wanted to do. After completing his service, Nicky returned to Bessemer where he began working full-time at the Bright Star. He has been there ever since.

While her brothers grew into their professional roles at the Bright Star, the restaurant affected Helen's life in a more personal way. It was at the Bright Star in 1962 that Helen met the man she would marry, John Constantine Cocoris. John remembered,

> My first visit to the Bright Star was when I was in college at the University of Alabama. I was hitchhiking back to Tuscaloosa with a friend and we decided to stop there to eat.
>
> My dad, Gus H. Cocoris, was good friends with the Koikos family. My dad and Mr. Pete Koikos had worked in the same restaurant across from the Morris Hotel on First Avenue in downtown Birmingham. When I came back from serving in the army in 1962, Dad told me that it was time for me to get married. I told him I hadn't really decided yet, and was deferring on the prospects for the present.
>
> He suggested that I go to Bessemer to meet the daughter of the Bright Star's owner. Dad had gone to reconnoiter the family and had liked what he had seen. I called for a date with Helen in January 1963. I remember that Nicky was there when I went to call.

John and Helen were engaged in April 1963 and married that November. "Our wedding was on November 24, 1963, just two days after President Kennedy had been killed," Helen recalled. "I remember we were unwrapping our wedding gifts when we heard about the assassination in Dallas. Imagine our horror when we heard on television, just as we were preparing for the wedding, that Jack Ruby had just shot Lee Harvey Oswald. I told my parents that no matter what else happened, we were getting married today!"

Updating the "Star"

Partly to commemorate the restaurant's sixtieth anniversary and partly to provide a needed facelift to the facility, the owners decided on a major renovation in 1966. Nicky Koikos recalled the plans the family made for the project.

> Everyone was excited. This was the largest renovation since the restaurant was moved into the new Realty Building in May 1915. The restaurant was closed April 1 through April 30, 1966. It was gutted to the walls in the dining room and kitchen. The octagon tile floor was covered with wall-to-wall carpet-

The Bright Star Café, March 31, 1966, the day before the restaurant closed for its first renovation. (Courtesy of the Koikos family.)

ing. The marble that covered the walls was replaced with an elegant wood. The plate glass windows at the front of the store were enclosed. The ceiling was slightly lowered and covered with acoustical tile. Angelos Petelos was the general contractor, and he agreed with Bill Koikos and Gus Sarris that the unique murals would remain. Chandeliers adorned the dining room. The kitchen floor was changed to quarry tile that had drains and could be easily cleaned, unlike the old worn cement floor. New, modern cooking equipment was installed. We added more booths, took out the long counter and put in a shorter one, and added more tables. We added space for about forty more people.

It was hailed as a complete transformation. The "Bessemer News" section of the Birmingham News commented on the project. An editor, Mr. Roger Thames, wrote that Bessemer had a restaurant with an atmosphere that could be in New York City.

This renovation did upgrade the dining experience for our patrons. Working conditions also improved for employees. While the restaurant was brought up to date, however, the work was more of a remodeling than a restoration. Certain original touches, such as the marble and tile floors, were lost.

Jimmy Koikos added, "I was pretty scared because we had budgeted $35,000. We ended up spending almost $48,000 on the work. It's part of what was needed to compete with other restaurants."

Nicky Koikos recalled the opening of a much-anticipated and, according to many, much-desired new amenity at the Bright Star.

"From 1915 until the late 1930s, the Bright Star Restaurant operated with only one restroom. This was reserved primarily for the ladies. Men were asked to go upstairs to the Realty Building, where many doctors, dentists, and lawyers had offices.

"There were two entrances for the patrons of the restaurant: one, facing Nineteenth Street, still exists today; the second, adjacent to the present-day ladies' room, connected the Bright Star to the lobby of the Realty Building. This second entrance was closed in 1939 to make room for a men's room. The era of the unisex restroom thankfully ended.

"Both of these restrooms, though kept clean and tidy, were cramped, with barely enough room to turn around. The heating system for the entire building passed through the walls of these restrooms. Customers would not linger. They would almost faint from the heat!

"Although the men's room was relocated in 1978 to the 1907 Room, female customers endured these close conditions until 1990. Space was acquired from a neighboring tenant to enlarge the ladies' room. Joy Toffel, an interior decorator from Birmingham, designed a more spacious, beautifully appointed area. Air conditioning was added! Corian countertops, high ceilings, and massive mirrors were introduced. It was quite a transformation!

"For a year or so after the remodeling, I would observe the expressions of the ladies who had suffered for over seventy years! It was fun seeing them open the door and gasp with delight. I laughed and they would look back at me and we both laughed together."

More Customer Recollections

The Bright Star's customers have generously shared memories of time spent at the restaurant in the 1960s. Tony B. Cacioppo, Jr., told of an annual Christmas shopping trip that culminated in a visit to the Bright Star.

> My cousins and some friends before Christmas would write our names on a piece of paper and put them in a hat. We each took turns drawing out the names. On a Saturday morning, we would get one of our parents to drive us to downtown Bessemer to shop at Kress or McClellan's department stores to buy a gift or toy for the person we drew. We had a limit of $2 to spend. This was around 1966.
>
> When we finished shopping, we would go to the Bright Star to eat lunch. A waitress would look at all of us kids and say, "Follow me," and take us past the kitchen to a booth with drawn curtains. There must've been around twelve kids, eight to twelve years of age. You should've seen the looks on all the customers' faces when we walked in with no adult supervision. . . . We ordered our meals and then exchanged gifts. When it came time to pay our bills, I remember my older cousins asking one person at a time, "How much money do you have?" Somebody would say $1.75, another would say $1.25, and another would say 85 cents. Finally, we got up enough to pay our bills.
>
> There at the register was Mr. Bill Koikos, Jimmy and Nick's father. Everyone that's been to the Bright Star knows there's a bowl of peppermint patties on the counter. This was some of my cousins' first time eating there and they were told that the restaurant gives away free candy after your meal and that Mr. Bill would ask, "You want a mint? You want a mint? A mint?" in his heavy Greek accent.
>
> Mr. Bill thanked us children for our business and saw some of the kids staring at the bowl full of peppermint patties. They were just waiting for those famous words to come out of Mr. Bill's mouth. When he finally realized what we were waiting on, he said, "You kids want a mint? A mint? Take a mint." You thought thousand-dollar bills were being handed out. All these hands dug into the bowl and took every one of those peppermint patties, with Mr. Bill's approval.

Lisa Warren Poole recalled what a special place the Bright Star was during her childhood. "Growing up in the 1960s and early 1970s and living approximately two miles from downtown Bessemer, my family and I were fortunate to frequent the Bright Star Restaurant just about every weekend," she reminisced.

Eating supper there was, I guess you could say, our Saturday night ritual. Although there was a wide variety of items on the menu to choose from, my mother and I usually had the fried shrimp and my father loved the hamburger steak smothered in onions and gravy. It was such a treat to eat there and even as a child I remembered getting the sense that it was really an upscale restaurant but yet the owners and employees stopped at our table frequently to talk with us and treated us like part of the family.

Sadly, when I became a teenager, I thought I was too old to go out to eat with my parents and I cheated myself out of many more wonderful dining experiences. If I had known then what I know now, I would have never passed up an opportunity to eat at the Bright Star! Many years have passed and the restaurant is larger in size than it was over thirty years ago, but the atmosphere, quality of food, and the attention given to serving the customers remain unchanged to this day.

The End of an Era

Other changes were taking place. In 1969, Gus Sarris, one of the two remaining second-generation partners, sold his interest in the Bright Star to Jimmy Koikos. The Bright Star would continue now under sole ownership of the Koikos family. Sarris died one year later at the age of sixty-eight.

"Uncle" Gus Sarris's death saddened the Bright Star family. Sarris had begun working at the Bright Star while still a youngster and had become more than a business partner. He had acted as a second father to his partner's son, John D. Bonduris, Jr. It is no exaggeration to say that this uniquely driven man, who left the Bright Star premises only to sleep or to take an afternoon nap, worked unceasingly to build the Bright Star into a successful business. He was considered a member of the family and had been a fixture in Bessemer for many years. His death on April 1, 1970, was mourned by all.

★6★

Rolling with the Changes

The 1970s

I love this place. I can't wait to get back here every day.

—Tasia Koikos

Hard Economic Times

After the social turmoil of the 1960s, Americans were anxious to restore order, confidence, and stability to their government, their foreign policy, and a shifting economy.

All of these would be slow in coming. There were continuing social and political crises with an escalation of domestic protest and social unrest, growing military frustration in Vietnam, a series of frightening and disorienting economic problems, and the Watergate scandal, which forced the resignation of President Nixon.

To make matters worse, an oil embargo imposed in 1973 by the Organization of Petroleum Exporting Companies (OPEC) led to rapidly rising oil pricing and long lines at gas stations. Americans were experiencing the worst energy crisis since World War II.

The picture in Bessemer was equally bleak, as businesses were anxious for the economy to regain its footing. In 1972 the Bessemer Chamber of Commerce identified 804 businesses and industries in the area, but their character had changed drastically since the days of the city's founding.

The mining and heavy manufacturing operations had all but shut down. In January 1970, four hundred miners joined the unemployment rolls as Woodward Iron Company closed down its mining operations at Muscoda and Pyne mines. The following November, the Woodward furnaces were targeted in the state's first major shutdown of some twenty-three companies in the Birmingham area during a major pollution crisis. The Environmental Protection Agency (EPA) went to federal court to force a number of manufacturers to cut back operations. Only one of the Woodward furnaces had remained in operation during the previous three months as the demand for pig iron, the only product of the blast furnaces, had dropped as a result of the utilization of scrap iron and foreign imports. Foreign iron and steel could be imported much more cheaply than those products could be produced at home.

On January 27, 1973, the last cast of iron from the old Woodward furnace was made, and the iron production division of the company closed after ninety years of continuous production. Mead Corporation, the parent company, began dismantling the venerable old plant.

The reliance on foreign imports further undermined the local economy. Citing unfairly priced imports and excessive environmental spending, U.S. Steel, long a major employer in Jefferson County, announced in 1979 the closing of ten of its plants nationwide. Parts of six other of the company's operations were shut down, and 13,000 workers were without jobs. The nation's biggest steel producer blamed the EPA for its predicament, particularly the $1.8 billion it had to spend to comply with clean air standards.

That pinch was also felt in Bessemer as many iron and steel workers found themselves looking for work. In addition, the Pullman plant had fallen on hard times. From a high mark of employment of 4,648 people in the early 1970s, the plant was put on life support as the financial recession worsened later in the decade. Orders for new railroad boxcars became almost nonexistent. Bessemer's glory days as an industrial center were coming to a close.

As is usually the case, however, the closing of one door signaled the opening of another. The city was about to embark on a diversification of its economic base and an aggressive growth initiative that would not put all its eggs into a single basket, as had been the case in the early days of the community.

New Influences

At the Bright Star, both the changing economic landscape and the leadership of Jimmy and Nicky Koikos resulted in changing clientele in the 1970s. Although the majority of customers were still Bessemer residents, especially at lunch, the restaurant began to gain a reputation for excellence with patrons from Birmingham and Tuscaloosa.

Ralph "Buddy" Armstrong, Bessemer's representative in the Alabama legislature from 1974 until 1978, sponsored a resolution in the House of Representatives to name the Bright Star one of the top five restaurants in the state. This publicity helped increase business at the restaurant. As well, enthusiastic comments from customers about the Bright Star's fresh seafood and delicious steaks awakened Jimmy Koikos to the possibility for the restaurant to become a statewide landmark.

Jimmy had begun visiting New Orleans at that time, and a friend from Bessemer, John Payne, recommended he visit Commander's Palace Restaurant. Jimmy followed John's advice and discovered the culinary delights for which Commander's Palace, one of the Big Easy's premier dining haunts, was known. Jimmy felt that the outstanding specialty dishes and fine dining atmosphere of Commander's Palace were similar in character to the culture of excellence that had become a trademark of the Bright Star. "When I started going down to New Orleans in the 1970s, I just realized what the quality of good food could do," Jimmy said in an interview that was published in *Tuscaloosa* magazine. "Commander's Palace is way out there on Washington Street, cemeteries and such around it, and yet people still find their way there."

Jimmy's continuing relationship with Commander's Palace led to the inception of the annual Taste of New Orleans weekend, a hugely successful occasion that began in the 1980s.

Remoulade Sauce

This is the Bright Star version of a New Orleans classic. Add more horseradish for a bigger kick.

3 stalks celery, pureed in blender and drained of water

2 cups regular mayonnaise
1/2 cup tomato ketchup
1/2 cup prepared horseradish
2 tablespoons paprika
1/4 teaspoon cayenne pepper
1/2 teaspoon white vinegar
juice of 1 lemon

Combine above ingredients in bowl and stir well. Refrigerate overnight before serving.

Makes 1 quart. Delicious on cold boiled shrimp or as a salad dressing.

New Direction in the Kitchen

Gus Sarris's five decades at the Bright Star had established a high standard of excellence for both the food coming out of the kitchen and the cooking habits and techniques used to produce it. He had developed dishes like Greek-style snapper and trout almondine, as well as the filleting technique used to process the fresh Gulf fish that he insisted on. After his retirement in 1969, a new chief was needed to maintain Gus's standards while keeping up with the Bright Star's growing clientele.

Meanwhile, Jimmy and Nicky as on-site owners were showing their respective talents in the management of the business. Jimmy was developing into a first-rate front man, with his natural ability to greet and chat with customers while simultaneously guiding them to their seats and making sure that their needs were met during their stay. In the back of the house, Nicky's attention to detail and genuine esprit

Lobster and Crabmeat Au Gratin

This rich seafood dish is wonderful as a main course with a fresh Greek salad on the side.

1 1/2 quarts whole milk
1/2 pound butter (2 sticks)
1 1/4 cup all-purpose flour
3 eggs, well beaten
1/2 cup sherry or white wine
2 1/4 cups Parmesan cheese, divided
1 pound lump crabmeat
1 pound steamed lobster pieces (small steamed shrimp may be substituted)
1/4 teaspoon white pepper
1/2 teaspoon paprika

Preheat oven to 350°. Butter a 3 1/2-quart baking dish. Heat milk in saucepan until hot (do not boil). Melt butter in large saucepan. Whisk in flour until roux is formed, stirring constantly. Slowly add hot milk to roux, whisking over low heat until mixture thickens. Pour thickened mixture into large bowl and stir in eggs until well blended. Add sherry, 2 cups Parmesan cheese, crabmeat, lobster, and white pepper. Pour mixture into baking dish. Sprinkle with remaining Parmesan cheese and paprika. Bake for 15–20 minutes at 350° until lightly browned.

Serves 10–12.

de corps with the staff created a "machine" for turning out consistently delicious plates of fresh seafood and steak in a timely manner. However, neither developed a taste for doing the actual cooking.

A man named Junius Harris, who had come to work at the Bright Star as a porter in 1957, stepped up to the challenge of upholding the Bright Star's reputation for excellence. Over the course of the 1960s, he had emerged as a protégé of Gus Sarris as Sarris moved toward retirement. Harris had a natural flair for cooking and excelled at the seafood and steak specialties that the public loved. Harris presided over his kitchen in a quiet but authoritative manner. He became adept at accommodating customer requests. Nita Ray Fitzgerald, a fixture at the Bright Star as a server from 1968 until 1996, remarked that he and she together came up with the Texas Special—portions of Greek-style snapper, Greek tenderloin, and lobster and crabmeat au gratin. This popular sampler platter was named for a Texas businessman who frequently visited the Bright Star as a guest of regulars John and Catherine Fievet.

Current Bright Star employees recalled the workings of the kitchen under Harris. "The place was busy for the size of it," said chef Walter Hoskins, who started at the Bright Star in 1967. "We had to do a lot of things. We had to cut up ham steaks, liver, and whole lambs, and cook whole turkeys and veal hind." Betty Bailey, who came to the Bright Star in 1970, added, "We had a small kitchen back then. I started out making salad dressing and tartar sauce from scratch—the French, Roquefort, Thousand Island—all the salad dressings are still made from scratch. Back in the 1970s, we didn't have as many people in the kitchen as we do now. We had a few people doing a lot of different things. We were very proud of the fact that we got the food out quickly and correctly to the customers. Today, there are many people doing very specialized jobs."

Harris left the Bright Star in 1983, having had a lasting effect on the way the Bright Star is run today. Walter Hoskins remembers that Harris taught him "a lot about the business, how to do the cooking, and how to maneuver around the kitchen." Kitchen administrator Carl Thomas, who started as a porter in 1975, says that what Harris taught him helped him gain his current position.

In the Public Eye

One of Jimmy Koikos's progressive moves at the Bright Star in the 1970s was to give the restaurant a higher public profile via newspaper and radio. He became friends with Dennis Washburn, who was a columnist at the *Birmingham News* from 1968 until 1991. "One night I was at the Cainbreak on the Southside Strip," remembered Jimmy. "I was talking to the owner, Bob Cain, and he suggested I introduce myself to Dennis Washburn. I went over to his table and told him who I was, and I invited him to come to the Bright Star for dinner. He came one night and enjoyed everything. Later, he wrote a review of the Bright Star for his 'Dining Out' column. Afterward we noticed a boost in our business from people coming from Anniston, Gadsden, Tuscaloosa, and other areas where the *News* was circulated. We

Illustration from Dennis Washburn's "Dining Out" column, 1972, reviewing the Bright Star. (Courtesy of the Cocoris family.)

became good friends with Dennis, and he wrote regularly about us." An extensive article Washburn wrote about Bill Koikos and his family for the *Birmingham News* on February 25, 1980, is excerpted in chapter 2 of this book. This four-page article, supplemented by photographs of the Koikos family and Bright Star employees, was one of the first to showcase the restaurant as a landmark.

Jimmy also became friends with the widely known radio personalities Tommy Charles and John Ed Willoughby. Both men liked the restaurant, and an advertising agreement with them was easy to negotiate. On their popular show *T. C. and John Ed in the Morning* heard on WSGN they would mention the Bright Star in both paid advertisements and off-the-cuff personal endorsements. Jimmy's contacts with Washburn and T. C. and John Ed helped boost the Bright Star into the notice of diners well beyond Bessemer.

Their Own "Miss America"

In the 1970s, Tasia Koikos, in addition to being "Yiayia" to Helen's three young daughters, became a fixture at the Bright Star. Often walking the mile or so from her home on Dartmouth Avenue, she joined her husband to open the restaurant early in the mornings for the chefs and food vendors. She oversaw deliveries and supervised the daily laundering of dishtowels, tablecloths, and napkins. During business hours, she could often be found at the water station, where she sliced lemons, filled water glasses, and brewed tea in huge kettles.

Sherry Parsons, a server, cashier, and hostess at the Bright Star from 1979 until 2003, recalled, "She took particular care in making tea. She would brew the tea herself, which was a forty-five-minute process. She used no machine. It was not until her death that a tea machine was purchased. Tasia was very hard-working. She would come in the morning to peel leftover baked potatoes for the next day's potato salad. She was not too big for any job."

Parsons added an anecdote that demonstrates Tasia's pride in "her" restaurant: "In the early 1980s, cherry trees were planted in the sidewalk outside the restaurant. She treated those trees like her own and watered them with a gallon bucket. Her husband used to fuss about it, but she had a sense of pride about them and loved to take care of the plants. I think of her when I see the cherry trees blossom every spring."

Jimmy Koikos contributed his own memories of his mother at the restaurant: "Mother worked here from 1969 until 1989. Some of the happiest days of my life were the days that my daddy and mother worked together at the Bright Star. They'd get up at around five o'clock in the morning and have their coffee while watching Country Boy Eddie on television. Sometimes we would have Mr. Willie, one of our employees, waiting outside the house to take them to work together."

Tasia's true joy, however, came from greeting customers in the restaurant. Like her husband, she loved visiting with friends and diners who became regulars at the Bright Star. Martha McClinton Langford told how her mother, one of these regular customers, was welcomed by Tasia.

> Every Thursday my mother, Margaret McClinton, my aunt Lucile Flynn, and two other lifelong friends (Maude Cowen and Florence Russell) would drive from Hueytown to the Bright Star. They were all retired teachers and were all "seniors."
>
> They would arrive before [the Bright Star] opened for lunch so they could find a close parking place. Mrs. Koikos would always meet them at the front door . . . sometimes letting them in early. She always greeted them with "I already have your decaf coffee ready." Her graciousness was a perfect beginning to a delicious lunch that they looked forward to for many, many years.

"Mama had a great relationship with everyone there," said Helen Koikos Cocoris. "She had certain male customers, notably Mr. Danny Hill, along with the milkman and the coffee rep, who were her 'boyfriends.' My mother loved to joke and to be with people who made her laugh. It made her feel good and made everyone else feel good, too, especially when the restaurant was in full swing."

Sherry Parsons recounted the genesis of a favorite running joke between Tasia and the servers: "She coined the nickname 'Miss America' for herself. One year she told me she was going to win the Miss America pageant and that the servers would all be behind her carrying her train when she won. From then on all the servers called her 'Miss America.' At her funeral, a banner on the wreath of flowers from the servers read 'Good-bye, Miss America.'"

Fortunate indeed was the person who received Tasia's ultimate token of her affection—a loaf of her delicious homemade bread. Jo Ann Barr of Bessemer wrote about visiting the Bright Star with her two young sons in the 1970s and eating Tasia's homemade bread as part of their meal. Similarly, Jane White Mulkin, a Bessemer native and good friend of Helen Koikos Cocoris, remembered Tasia "bringing slices of her warm homemade bread to the table." Nita Ray Fitzgerald recalled that Tasia also made a delicious meat sauce that was served in the restaurant.

Daughter Helen summed up Tasia's feelings for the Bright Star: "I asked her one day why she wanted to spend so much time at the restaurant. I said, 'Mother, your kids are fine and the Bright Star is doing well. You don't have to be at the restaurant that much.' She replied indignantly, 'Are you crazy? I love this place. I can't wait to get back here every day.'"

Bill Koikos and sons at the Bright Star, 1978. (Courtesy of the Cocoris family.)

"Mr. Bill" Turns Eighty

Having started as a busboy in 1920, Bill Koikos remained a constant presence at the Bright Star even after his eightieth birthday in 1974. When the Bright Star incorporated that year, Bill officially transferred ownership to his sons, Jimmy and Nicky. He continued to work as cashier at the restaurant daily, and as the decade wore on, he worked mainly during the slower periods between lunch and dinner. According to Angie Sellers, who worked as a cashier, server, and hostess from 1977 until 2002, "he would do anything from cashier to wash windows."

Employees and customers remember Bill Koikos for his unfailing gentlemanliness. He continued to take great pride in his appearance by dressing every day in a suit, tie, and freshly pressed shirt, topped by a fedora. He also enjoyed the spectacle of attractively dressed waitresses, recalled server Nita Ray Fitzgerald: "Nicky had ordered us these short, green dresses to wear, and I felt like I don't know what. I was standing at the door, and Mr. Bill was admiring me and saying, 'Miss Nita, you're so cute!' Then another waitress walked in and Mr. Bill came out from behind the register and said to her, 'You look so good, you so pretty . . . but your dress is too long!' She had made a green ruffle and put it on this dress to lengthen it, but he said, 'That ruffle doesn't go!'"

Although he had reached a level of material comfort unimaginable to him in his youth, Bill never lost a profound sense of thankfulness for all that he had. His daughter remembers that he often paused in front of the iconostasis in his home to say a quick prayer. The success of the Bright Star, especially under his sons' direction, always astonished him. When Jimmy would tell his father the number of customers served on a busy day, he would reply, "Don't tell anybody! They'll call you a liar!"

Bill continued to train cashiers during this period, bringing his habitual neatness to the task. Granddaughter Connie Cocoris Chwe recalled his insistence on having all the bills in the cash register drawer facing the same way. Sherry Parsons remembered that he was very picky about the management of the cash register. "The first time I cashed, he watched over my shoulder and made sure I counted the cash back correctly," she recalled. "It made me very nervous. After that first time, he had confidence in me and never watched me again. He never learned to use the credit card machine, though—he used to always call me to the front to run it."

Although his prevailing characteristic was sweetness, Bill was known to lose his temper when provoked. Two longtime Bright Star employees gave examples of this rare, but memorable, occurrence. "One day Mr. Bill was counting his money at the register," remembered Carl Thomas, a thirty-year veteran of the Bright Star. "I told him I needed a key to let the bread man in. He got angry and told me I had made him lose his place. He ended up getting me a key so that I wouldn't have to bother him again."

Nita Ray Fitzgerald told of that quick temper coming to her rescue.

> There was a man who worked at a retail store close by who used to come in every day. One night he came in and had too much to drink. I had just poured him a vodka on the rocks and had begun to serve another customer, when he began to curse at me. Mr. Bill was furious. He walked over to that customer with the white napkin he always carried and popped it hard on the counter in front of him. He said, "You get out of here now! Don't talk to her like that! She doesn't have to take that off of you, and you don't come here for your vodka anymore!" He was the sweetest, most gentle man, but when he lost his temper, you knew it!

Bill and Tasia's time of "active retirement" in the 1970s was characterized by the pleasure they took in simply enjoying the restaurant and the people they visited with every day. As Mitch Abercrombie, owner of White's Hardware Store down the street from the restaurant, said, "I always remember that Mr. Bill had a quiet dignity about himself. We have operated a store down the street for about forty years, and Miss Tasia and Mr. Bill would always bring us coffee in the mornings. I treasure those memories 'til this day."

Memories of the "Bear"

Always fervent supporters of the Alabama Crimson Tide, Jimmy and Nicky got into the spirit of football season in the 1970s by having their waitresses don jersey-like tunics in the colors of both the Alabama and Auburn teams on weekends. Current server Rita Weems remembered, "Each server had an Alabama jersey and an Auburn jersey and you were supposed to rotate them. One Alabama and Auburn game, Alabama won, and I was supposed to wear my Auburn jersey. I did, but I was the only one. All the other servers wore their Alabama uniforms. I was so mad! One Auburn fan eating at the restaurant asked to see me as I was the only Auburn server that night. I said no, I don't want to! I am an Alabama fan!"

The Bright Star's increase in business became evident on the Saturday nights when Alabama played a home game, when, as server Sherry Parsons remembered, guests lined up around the block to get into the restaurant. The crowds were such that the supply of rolled silverware often ran out, and the servers had to rush to roll more.

Longtime server and server manager Myrtle Williams recalled an apex of football craziness: one night the constant flow of customers became so intense that when one inebriated patron passed out in a booth with her feet extending into the aisle, the servers and hosts simply stepped over the obstruction and carried on.

Jimmy and Nicky were thrilled to see football players, past and present, and coaches from the University of Alabama begin to frequent the Bright Star—notably Bart Starr, Johnny Musso, Major Ogilvie, and especially the "Bear." During his heyday, Coach Paul "Bear" Bryant often came to the restaurant to enjoy a bit of privacy in one of the back booths.

Jimmy Koikos shared several memories of the "Bear" and the Bright Star.

> Daddy wasn't a big football fan, but I was always interested in the sport. When I was a junior in high school, I remember going to Mobile to see Coach Bryant's first game. Later, I went to Memphis to see his last game. I followed him through his entire career. The man knew exactly what to say and when to say it. He was a master at motivating people.

I remember one Monday night in the 1970s before our expansion, I got a telephone call from a man who wanted to make reservations for two for dinner. I told him that since it was a Monday evening, we would not be full. He could just come by at his convenience.

He again told me that he wanted to reserve a private booth for two people. I told him that our booths are reserved for eight or more guests, but to just come by, ask for Jimmy, and I would be glad to accommodate him.

He proceeded to tell me that he wanted a private booth for two with a television.

I said, "Sir, may I ask who is requesting a private booth for two people with a television?"

He said, "This is Bear Bryant."

I said, "You've got it, Coach." I ran home, took my mother's television set out of her house, returned to the restaurant, and set it up in a private booth in the back. Coach Bryant wanted to come for dinner and watch Monday Night Football.

I also remember driving by one night when I wasn't working and seeing a huge crowd. I thought, "Wow, Nicky's really got a crowd in there tonight." But I wondered why the television was being played so loudly that I could hear it out in the street. I went inside and turned the set down and asked why it was so loud. Someone said it was because Coach Bryant wanted it loud. I walked right back over there and turned it up again. Coach and Mrs. Bryant and several of their friends were eating there that night.

Another time, I walked out onto the practice field in Tuscaloosa to watch the team work out. Coach was sitting on a golf cart. It was really hot that day. I said, "Coach, how are you?" He looked at me and said, "What are you doing here? Every time I see you I get hungry."

He was a wonderful coach and a real motivator. It was a real pleasure to talk to a man like that. I came to understand that if you run a business the way he ran a football team, you'd have a pretty successful business.

One time I asked him how it was that he was consistently winning SEC titles and competing for the national championship. He said, "You give me a ballplayer who will give you 110 percent effort, as opposed to a player who will give you 100 percent effort, and I'll win you a national championship."

SAPS in the 1970s

An informal group, characterized by coffee consumption and spirited political discourse, began meeting daily at the Bright Star in the late 1930s. The Solve All Problems Society (SAPS) met at the Bright Star for breakfast originally, and in the afternoon when the restaurant stopped serving breakfast. An article written in 1979 by Danny Ausbun for the Metro Section of the *Birmingham News* describes this organization and its unofficial scope of work.

> Virtually every restaurant in almost every city has its "coffee-drinkers' table," and Bessemer is no different.
>
> But the big table at the Bright Star Restaurant even has a semi-official name: SAPS.
>
> The Solve All Problems Society was given its mock-serious name by the late Roger Thames, editor of The Bessemer News and a regular there for many years.
>
> Ask any of the regulars if he is a "sap" and he'll probably tell you that the rest of the men are, but he isn't.
>
> Headquartered in the back corner of the restaurant, the SAPS assembly runs just about continuously from 8 to 10 a.m. daily. Nobody ever stays at the table the entire time, but the talkers wander in and out as their schedules permit. At any given time, there will be from four to a dozen men at the two pushed-together tables.
>
> Some of the retired members have plenty of time to relish the tall tales, sports stories, jokes, serious and not-so-serious discussions, and ribbing of other members—standard fare on any given morning.
>
> The table also is frequented by businessmen, politicians, and sometimes even a minister bold enough to sit down.
>
> County Commission President Tom Gloor, making an infrequent visit a couple of weeks ago, was discussing state politics when he said, "I can't stand those politicians."
>
> When somebody pointed out that Gloor is a politician, he responded, "I think of myself as a statesman."
>
> That type of banter is typical of the morning SAPS conclaves, where almost nothing is too trivial for lengthy discussion.
>
> About the only function of the SAPS, other than to entertain each other and consume substantial quantities of coffee, is to have an annual Christmas party. There, you can see that when all of those claiming SAPS membership get together at once, they probably number 100. The party fills almost every table at the Bright Star.

Ed Kean, age eighty-seven, a member of SAPS since its inception, added these reminiscences of the club.

When I started attending SAPS in the late 1930s, Mr. Gus [Sarris] was the cook. In those days we came through the kitchen because I worked at McDonald's Furniture, which was behind the Bright Star. Can't imagine the Health Department allowing something like that today.

One afternoon, Mr. John Vines, a regular SAPS member, was eating a piece of pie. Mr. Henry Sweet, another regular, bet John he could not eat one whole pie. When he was down to the last couple of pieces of a lemon icebox pie, John realized he couldn't do it. He saw another SAPS member leave to go to the bathroom and followed him. He asked the friend, who worked at the courthouse, to have one of his colleagues call the Bright Star and pretend he was [then governor] George Wallace [Henry was active in Wallace's reelection campaign]. When Henry ran excitedly to take the call, John distributed the remaining pieces of pie to other SAPS members to finish for him. When Henry returned from "speaking with the governor," the pie was gone and he had to pay for it. He good-naturedly did, and it remained a joke for many years.

Eddie Dunlavy remembers another story about SAPS.

In March 1963 the SAPS was having its usual discourse when they heard a loud siren up front. At the same time, they observed the kitchen doors and the front doors swing open. They raced from the coffee table to the front of the restaurant just in time to see pieces of tin roofing fly down Nineteenth Street. A tornado had hit downtown Bessemer!

The men ran back inside and got under the coffee table. At the same time, several pieces of the ceiling fell off and some bricks fell down through the opening. All the men were scared that the roof would blow off. One man had the presence of mind to reach for his beer and bring it under the table. No one was hurt, thank goodness, but the man with the beer, who requested anonymity, remained the butt of jokes for years.

Kean lamented that there are only a few of the old-timers left now. "It's been a lot of fun over the years," he said. Or, as Danny Ausbun concluded in his *Birmingham News* article, "Just like there will always be an England, Bessemer's downtown people will always congregate somewhere to drink coffee and solve the problems of the world at the beginning of the day. So the spirit of the SAPS will undoubtedly go on forever."

Spreading Out

With its higher profile attracting more and more diners, especially on weekends, the Bright Star was ready for its first significant expansion. The 1966 remodeling had reconfigured and redecorated the original 1915 space; now more square footage would be added at the rear of the restaurant.

In late 1977, Nicky Koikos noticed that a loan company had vacated a section of the Realty Building that faced Third Avenue. He determined that this space would meet the existing restaurant with enough of an overlap to provide an opening between them. The fit seemed perfect for the expansion of the Bright Star.

The new dining room, called the 1907 Room, was designed and constructed in 1978 by Angelos Petelos to be a smaller replica of the main dining room. The famous octagon mosaic tile floor was reproduced in the new dining areas. Its row of private booths, divided by retractable partitions, was given a turn-of-the-century look by transoms of brass rail and stained glass. Stained glass panels featuring the Bright Star logo accented the smaller, open booths opposite the row of private booths. Enlarged black-and-white photographs of historic Bessemer sites decorated the upper walls. A larger men's room and an additional ladies' room were also added.

Nicky noted that the best part of the new dining room's layout was its proximity to the kitchen. The increased flow from the kitchen, which was also slightly altered at this time, did not interfere with traffic to the main dining room. The Bright Star now had a seating capacity of 155 diners. Tom Bonduris, who had died only a few years before in Greece, would have been proud to see this addition to his Bright Star.

The combination of increased publicity and physical expansion helped the Bright Star gain even greater recognition during the 1970s as Bessemer looked to a new era economically—one that would eventually bring it to nationwide prominence.

★7★

Up, Up, and Away

The 1980s

Jimmy and Nicky were always good at putting money back into the business.
—Tommy Finley

Economic Recovery

The hard economic times of the 1970s slowly gave way to recovery and prosperity. President Ronald Reagan took office in 1981 with a call to Congress for an unprecedented shrinkage of domestic spending. In his message to Congress of February 8, 1982, he advocated putting "the false prosperity of overspending, easy credit, depreciating money, and financial excess behind us" and vowed to "shun retreat, [and] to weather the temporary dislocations and pressures that must inevitably accompany the restoration of national economic, fiscal, and military health."

Reagan's policies turned the economy around, but the result was an America with a new look. Beset by competition from abroad, U.S. manufacturing gave way to service and retail industries. The AFL-CIO lamented the erosion of America's industrial base as manufacturing fell from 30 percent of the country's gross national product in 1953 to just 21 percent twenty years later. By 1986, service industries had created ten million jobs nationwide while 1.5 million were lost in manufacturing.

This trend from a manufacturing to a service economy began in Bessemer with the closing of the Pullman-Standard boxcar plant on September 28, 1981. The world's largest railcar plant, which for years had been the city's largest employer, was no more. Fifty square blocks in the heart of Bessemer were suddenly vacant. The bustling plant where the company's millionth boxcar had been built less than two years before was quiet.

However, there was a partial resurgence later in the decade. Texas-based Trinity Industries reopened the old Pullman facility in 1985 and employed 900 people, or about 25 percent of its former workforce. It would continue producing railroad boxcars until it closed for good in 1997.

The Hercules Powder plant, another of the city's major employers, closed its doors in the 1980s, further adding to the economic woes of the city. Bessemer's unemployment rate, which had hovered at 15–20 percent at the beginning of the recession, soared as high as 35 percent during the 1980s. Bessemer's once vibrant downtown deteriorated into a series of dilapidated, vacant storefronts. Following the 1980 census, Bessemer lost its designation as a central city.

To battle the decline of Bessemer's industrial base, an enthusiastic downtown redevelopment effort began in the mid-1980s spearheaded by Jim Byram, the executive director of the Bessemer Industrial Board, and his assistant, Troy Post. They were joined by Jeff Traywick, economic development specialist with the city's community and economic development unit. The Bessemer Area Chamber of Commerce would also play a leading role in forging a new business climate in the city.

The Industrial Development Board (IDB) and the chamber of commerce began wooing businesses of varying types and sizes to the area. They were aided by infrastructure improvements that came with the growth of western Jefferson County. The completion of interstate connector 459 offered Bessemer as an attractive location for corporate and light industrial parks. Whereas in 1983 Bessemer had just two industrial or business parks, the city would boast fifteen by 2002. In addition, state highway 150 was becoming a vital connector from Bessemer to the growing city of Hoover.

Using economic incentives, the IDB encouraged new businesses to relocate to the region and provided them with information about the community, available property, and buildings. Attractive new residential neighborhoods sprang up. By the time the city was celebrating its one-hundredth anniversary in 1987, Bessemer was well on its way to diversifying its economy and actively courting the hospitality and attractions industries. Since 1987, the city has added 2,500 new jobs, more than $105 million in new capital investment, and more than four million square feet of new construction or renovation.

Back to New Orleans

At the Bright Star, the creation of the 1907 Room and the restaurant's higher public profile led to a habitually busy restaurant, with hungry customers filling the expanded dining rooms to overflowing on Sundays and holidays. Customers would often wait on the sidewalk outside at these busiest times, even on rainy days and in the hot Alabama summers. Employee Angie Sellers remembered that Jimmy Koikos would send her outside with a pot of coffee or pitcher of iced tea to serve the people waiting in line.

A dining innovation that began in the mid-1980s grew from Jimmy Koikos's friendship with Jamie Shannon, the head chef of Commander's Palace, and with its owners, the Brennan family in New Orleans. Jamie had been a personal chef to Donald Trump and was known for his culinary genius.

Tommy Finley, who worked as general manager at the Bright Star from 1985 until 1994, remembers the first meeting with Shannon. "Jimmy and I went to New Orleans and were talking to George Rico [the late maitre d' of Commander's Palace]," he recalled. "Emeril Lagasse was the executive chef at Commander's then. George told us that Emeril wasn't in, but that we should meet the sous-chef, Jamie Shannon. Jamie sat down with us and I asked, 'Would you come to the Bright Star and cook?' He said yes."

Shannon and Jimmy Koikos planned a weekend of special dinners called a Taste of New Orleans, during which Shannon would prepare several of his signature dishes in the Bright Star's kitchen. Finley continued the story.

> When he came [the first time, in 1986] he made barbequed shrimp and bread pudding. He came by himself. We had no idea how well we would do. Jamie did not understand the amount of business the Bright Star normally did anyway. When we did a little advertising, it was a killer. We went through five hundred pounds of shrimp the first night.
>
> Jamie came back the next year. He found out when he was visiting the Bright Star that he'd been made executive chef at Commander's after Emeril left.
>
> The next year he let [current chef] Robert Moore and me come and cook for a week and work the various departments. We got great ideas from that.

The event proved immensely popular and was always a sellout. Jimmy and Nicky decided to begin offering to the Bright Star's customers many of the fine dishes inspired by Jamie Shannon's recipes. Soon, the Koikos version of the Commander's Palace bread pudding was on the Bright Star's menu. Special New Orleans sauces were available on many of their seafood dishes. Zesty Creole and Cajun dishes joined the traditional Greek-style fare the Bright Star's customers had grown to love over the years.

Ross Daidone, general manager at the Bright Star for the last seven years, shared some good memories of Jamie Shannon's visits to the Star.

> Some of my most memorable moments here were our "Taste of New Orleans" evenings. It was a real pleasure to work with the late Jamie Shannon and his staff. Sometimes they would bring their own

Commander's Palace chef Kevin Ortner, Bright Star executive chef Rick Daidone, Commander's Palace executive chef Jamie Shannon, and Bright Star general manager Tommy Finley during the Taste of New Orleans weekend of 1992. (Courtesy of the Cocoris family.)

ingredients and sometimes they would have us order items for them. Jamie would use some of his own staff and some of ours.

Those evenings were fun, and our people all worked well together. Their Commander's Palace grouper, bananas foster, blackened snapper, and prime rib with crabmeat were especially popular dishes.

Rick Daidone, Ross's brother and executive chef at the Bright Star from 1990 until 2002, recalled other new dishes: "Over the twelve years that Jamie Shannon visited the Bright Star, he always brought new dishes and specialties. He introduced us to snapper Lyonnaise, oysters Commander's, remoulade sauce, and strawberry shortcake. He was a great personality. He knew his way around the kitchen very well and always used fresh ingredients. Jamie always knew how to work hard and how to play hard."

Austin Davis, whose mother, Jessie, has been a cherished caregiver and friend to the Koikos family for over thirty years, joined the Bright Star team as executive dinner chef in 1999. He echoes the Daidones' impressions: "[Jamie] had a positive influence on our employees. He increased the pride of our employees

Bright Star's New Orleans–Style Bread Pudding with Whiskey Sauce

This festive dessert must be made well in advance of suppertime—note the long period required to let the egg-rich pudding mixture cook to perfection. Adapted from Jamie Shannon, former chef de cuisine at Commander's Palace.

2 cups granulated sugar
2 tablespoons ground cinnamon
1 tablespoon ground nutmeg
12 eggs
1 quart heavy whipping cream
1 tablespoon pure vanilla extract
10 slices of French bread, cut in half
1/2 cup raisins

Preheat oven to 300°. Thoroughly butter a 3-quart baking dish. In a small mixing bowl, blend sugar, cinnamon, and nutmeg. Mix with spatula or wire whisk. Set aside. In a medium mixing bowl, whisk 12 eggs. Add whipping cream and vanilla extract and mix well. Slowly blend sugar mixture into egg mixture.

Place French bread halves into bottom of baking dish and sprinkle with raisins. Pour prepared mixture over bread and raisins. Let mixture soak into bread for about 10 minutes.

To bake:

Submerge pan in a water bath and bake at 300° for approximately 3 hours untilgolden brown and firm.

Note: Instead of raisins, fresh peaches or strawberries may be substituted. Serve with whiskey sauce (see below).

Serves 8–10.

Whiskey Sauce

2 cups half & half
1/2 cup sugar
1 teaspoon pure vanilla extract
1/2 teaspoon cornstarch, dissolved in
1 tablespoon water
2 tablespoons bourbon

In a saucepan, mix half & half, sugar, and vanilla. Bring to a gentle boil over medium heat. Add dissolved cornstarch and stir until slightly thickened. Add bourbon and stir. Serve over bread pudding.

Jessie Davis and her son, Bright Star executive chef Austin Davis, 2006. Jessie Davis worked as a full-time caretaker for Bill Koikos toward the end of his life as part of her nearly forty years of friendship with the Koikos and Cocoris families. (Courtesy of the Cocoris family.)

and that improved the quality of the food and of the restaurant. He had charisma. When you could work 600–700 covers, you felt good about what you'd accomplished. He was a great inspiration."

Jimmy commented further on his association with Jamie Shannon, who died in November 2001, in an interview in 2006. "Jamie Shannon was an incredibly talented person and a good friend," Jimmy noted. "We really enjoyed having him come here for the special Commander's Palace nights. In addition to his skills in the kitchen, he also had a wonderful knack for the business side of running a restaurant. And he was a first-rate guy. He'd be all business for twelve hours in the kitchen, but then he'd sit down and have fun with you after he was through working. Losing him to cancer at such a young age was a real tragedy."

A Taste of New Orleans continues to be a well-attended event. Chef Jared Tees, a protégé of Jamie Shannon and chef at New Orleans' Restaurant Lüke, continues Jamie's tradition by headlining the event each year.

Strengthening Their Roots

Another phase of the Bright Star's history began in 1982, when the Koikos brothers purchased the Realty Building. This move gave the brothers complete control over the space that their restaurant had occupied for almost eighty years. Jimmy recalled,

> We bought the Realty Building from Wallace Boothby. Selling the building was a really tough decision for him to make. The day we bought the building was one of the happiest days of my life in the business world. It allowed us to do what we wanted to do with the business.
>
> I remember the advice I got from Charles Stephens, the brother of the late Rodger Stephens, my best friend and my partner in a hotel in Florida. Charles came in the restaurant one day and told me that if we ever got a chance to buy the building we should do it. With ownership of the building, I felt we could expand like we wanted to do.
>
> We bought the building with assistance from a government grant and renovated the upper three floors. It was solidly built of brick and cement, and featured quality construction throughout. It remains fully occupied with tenants today.

Nicky Koikos detailed the transformation of the Realty Building: "The building was gutted to the concrete shell. We put in a new elevator and completely redid the lobby. New plumbing, heating, and air conditioning were installed. A new electrical system was put in. Since the building is listed on the National Register of Historic Places, the windows could not be changed. The building's tenants today are lawyers, mortgage companies, accountants, and government offices."

Jimmy Koikos added, "My mom used to say that if Nicky hadn't gone into the restaurant business, he would have been an engineer. He had a lot of input into the remodeling we did. He could see things that we couldn't see."

In 1984, Jimmy and Nicky took over the retail space adjacent to their restaurant that had been vacated by South Central Bell. The area had the same dimensions as the original Bright Star—twenty-five by one hundred feet. This space was remodeled into two new dining rooms, capable of seating very large parties, plus a small waiting area that doubled as a service bar. The new dining rooms were called the Green Room (simply because of the color of its walls) and the Dixie Room. The latter took its name from the local Nissan dealership owned by the late Charles Campbell. His wife, Betty, recalled that Dixie Datsun (as Nissan was known at the time) wanted to use the unfinished dining room for a large party. Jimmy Koikos moved tables and chairs in for their event, and from then on the room was called the Dixie Room.

Exterior of the Realty Building, 2006. (Courtesy of the Cocoris family.)

Tommy Finley recalled adjusting to serving banquet-sized groups.

> We got into the banquet business when U.S. Steel requested that the Bright Star accommodate large departmental management parties. We had to learn how to do the big parties along with regular business. We expanded the kitchen and added another food line. One line was set up for the dining rooms. A second line was set up for the banquet rooms.
>
> Jimmy and Nicky were always good at putting money back into the business. Jimmy was always for remodeling and getting good equipment to work with.

Nicky Koikos said of the remodeling, "Banquet facilities for as many as one hundred provided the opportunity to entertain rehearsal dinners, reunions, business meetings, and fraternal and sports organizations. Actual weddings have taken place in the restaurant. Although the total seating in the Bright Star exceeded three hundred with this addition, it became more relaxed and less hurried. A small waiting room was provided, which proved to be inadequate during busy times. It was an improvement, however, to being outside and enduring the elements."

Nicky Koikos in expanded Bright Star kitchen facilities, 1982. (Courtesy of the Cocoris family.)

Jimmy Koikos added, "When chain restaurants became popular in the 1980s, we had to make a number of changes to remain competitive. A number of people thought we were crazy to be spending a great deal of money to remodel and expand, but we felt we had to do it. It made us a complete restaurant. I feel that time has proven us right. Since the remodeling, we have been able to accommodate parties of six to one hundred people. The largest we've had was around 120."

Tommy Finley noted that "Jimmy and Nicky were smart to buy the Realty Building when they had the chance. If someone else owned the property, the rent would likely be so high that they could not stay there."

Changes in the Kitchen

As in the 1970s, the addition of more dining space, combined with continued media publicity, brought

Squash Casserole

Use your own home steamer to prepare the squash for this savory casserole. Cooks Marie Jackson and Betty Bailey developed this recipe in the 1990s.

5 medium squash (washed, scraped, and sliced)
1 medium onion, chopped

Preheat oven to 325º. Spray a 9 x 9 pan with nonstick cooking spray. Place squash and onion in a pot and add water to cover. Bring to a boil and simmer for 20 minutes (or until tender). Drain and place in mixing bowl.

Combine the following ingredients in a separate bowl:

1 1/2 teaspoons salt
1/4 teaspoon white pepper
5 eggs, beaten
1/2 teaspoon flavor enhancer, such as Accent
1 cup milk
1 1/3 cups flour
1/4 cup diced red peppers
1/2 cup Parmesan cheese
1/2 stick butter, melted

Fold mixture gently into squash and pour into prepared pan. Sprinkle additional 1/4 cup Parmesan cheese over top. Bake at 325º for 20 minutes.

Serves 8–10.

still larger crowds to the Bright Star in the 1980s. The Koikos brothers continued advertising on the radio and in newspapers; they also received regular, positive reviews in the local media such as *Southern Living* magazine. Jimmy maintained his ties to Tuscaloosa, developing a friendship with Alabama head coach Ray Perkins, who succeeded "Bear" Bryant after his death in 1983.

Tommy Finley related that during his nine years at the Bright Star, the number of weekday diners increased from about 250 to about 450. Diners, newly aware of the health benefits of fish, loved the fresh seafood at the Bright Star, which was not available at many restaurants. Nick Costas, who worked as the first non-family-member manager at the Bright Star from 1982 until 1995, made a major contribution to keeping the restaurant supplied with fresh fish by driving to Florida weekly to visit a local supplier there. He worked Friday, Saturday, and Sunday at the restaurant, then drove to Panama City and back, sometimes in one day, to bring a fresh catch to the restaurant. Tommy Finley joked, "Guests would come from Florida to get fresh fish at the Bright Star."

In 1983 Junius Harris left the Bright Star, and after two years during which Nicky oversaw the kitchen, James Veitch took over in that capacity. Although he stayed only three years, Veitch brought notable innovations to his kitchen: he brought lamb back onto the Bright Star's menu, added new pie recipes, and introduced a vegetable steamer to his equipment lineup. The red beans and rice that Veitch introduced from his native Louisiana is still offered at the Bright Star on Tuesdays for lunch.

Jimmy with longtime Bright Star employee Angie Sellers, 1999. (Courtesy of the Koikos family.)

In the Trenches

Several members of the Bright Star's waitstaff have shared amusing stories about their experiences in the 1980s. Angie Sellers, a war bride from Bristol, England, who worked as a cashier, server, and hostess for twenty-five years, recalled,

> One day I was asked to work at the cash register for awhile. I told Nicky I was terrible with money, but he told me it would just be for a short time. I had already poured coffee into a man's gumbo cup, so I figured maybe it was time for me to leave as a server! An elderly gentleman was paying his bill, which totaled around eighty dollars. He handed me a twenty-dollar bill. I said, "Sir, I think you owe a little more." He asked me how much, and when I told him, his pants fell down! He was so embarrassed standing there in his underwear! I don't think it was the amount of the bill that shocked him; I think he had been to the restroom and had not fastened his pants correctly.

Sherry Parsons remembered one particularly noteworthy Sunday night on her shift.

> [Auburn University] Coach Pat Dye visited the restaurant with a large party. They were the only ones that night in the 1907 Room, and I waited on them.
>
> I was trying to carry an armful of salads, and I tripped—one plate rolled right down the floor of the 1907 Room and made a lot of racket. Salad flew out everywhere! I was so embarrassed about the loud noise, and Jimmy came back and fussed at me.
>
> I never will forget that Pat Dye put his arm around my shoulder and said, "Don't worry about it. It's no big deal. Pressure is when there's forty-five seconds left in the fourth quarter and your team is behind by seven points!" I felt so relieved—I knew everything was going to be okay.

Sherry also recalled that legendary NASCAR driver Bobby Allison, his race team, and his sons Clifford and Davey came in regularly on Sunday night to eat after a race. Penny Allison, the wife of Eddie Allison, Bobby Allison's brother, wrote, "Bobby would call the Bright Star and Jimmy and Nicky would always wait for them to get there and serve them, no matter how late." Sherry remembered visits from racecar drivers Neil Bonnett and Red Farmer, and singer-actor Jimmy Dean as well.

The New Generation

In the 1980s, Helen Koikos Cocoris's three daughters were teenagers and occasionally helped at the restaurant. Stacey Cocoris Craig shared her memories of working at the Bright Star with her grandparents and uncles.

> I remember starting to work at the Bright Star when I was fourteen years old, in 1979. I would arrive on Sundays at my grandparents' house to spend the night, and I would spend Monday, Tuesday, and Wednesday at the Bright Star working in the summertime. I would accompany my grandparents to the restaurant, and we worked a "split shift," which means we worked lunch, took a two- or three-hour break, then returned for the dinner shift. (We generally did not close the restaurant, but worked until 7:30 or 8 p.m.) I remember my grandmother cutting radishes and lemons in a back booth and filling ice in glasses for iced tea and water. I started work as a "butter girl," delivering butter and waters to the table, progressing to a hostess and finally to cashier. My grandfather and Sherry Parsons taught me to count change. I also learned to roll silver from Myrtle Williams. The restaurant was considerably smaller at that time (it was before the Dixie and Green rooms were added), and I remember how busy it was.

People would be standing at the door waiting to be seated. I remember working as fast and as hard as I could to deliver the water, butter, and tea to our guests.

When I was in college, I would work on holidays and summer vacations. I worked as a cashier and hostess, particularly on Sundays and during special events like a Taste of New Orleans. I took great pride in working at the restaurant.

My grandparents were terrific role models for me. Though they were not educated and did not speak English as a first language, they instilled in me the value of hard work and the notion of customer service. My grandmother was a career woman before her time and encouraged my love of business. My grandfather would always offer our guests a chocolate mint as they exited the restaurant. Our guests loved him for that gesture.

They were very generous people and very humble. My grandparents were always available to help at the restaurant and took a sincere interest in and were very respectful of the restaurant's employees.

Connie Cocoris Chwe remembered the restaurant in her own way.

The Bright Star was, of course, part of our world from the very beginning. It was where we would go to see our mom's family. First, adorable Papou, who called us "Dahly" (for darling) and "Pooty" (for pretty) and handed out five-dollar bills from his money clip just because. We loved to pat him and hug him, and we called ourselves the Papou Fan Club because we liked to just sit and listen to him. He taught me how to make change and how to tidy the rows of cigarette packages and candy bars during lulls in the flow of customers. Then there was Yiayia, who could never hug or kiss us enough, or brag on us enough to hapless Bright Star customers. She really loved the customers, and after explaining to them how well we'd done on our last report card or where we were enrolled in college, she'd find something to laugh about with them. She had running jokes with everybody. Uncle Jimmy's amazing ability to pay attention to about seven things all at once meant that he could listen to whatever you were saying while also noticing that the folks in booth 20 needed iced tea and the ones in 23 were waiting for their check. During slow times, we loved to play paper football with him on the empty tables (though Sherry Parsons hated to have to pick up after us!). He threw us around as small children and taught us to throw a football and to drive a car (steering wheel only) long before it was legal. Uncle Nicky is more reserved than Uncle Jimmy but perhaps the most hilarious of all. His dry wit finds the humor in every situation, and when his laugh rings out, you laugh all the harder with him.

The waitresses were the epitome of efficiency and accomplishment. How I wanted to be like Billie

Hanson, with whom I often worked behind the cash register. She allowed me to run credit cards or make change, but it was clear that she didn't really need any help—she was so fast, and she could make conversation with each customer to boot! Many customers didn't believe that I could make change properly (I guess I was about fourteen or so), and one of them gave me a one-hundred-dollar bill for a check of less than ten dollars just to see what I would do. Of course, thanks to my training from Papou and Billie, I managed it.

I loved palling around with Sherry Parsons and Angie Sellers, who always made me laugh. I acted as hostess occasionally, but I lacked the polish of Billie, Sherry, and Angie, who seemed to be everyone's friend. Being at the Bright Star was fantastic training for working with people and meeting the public.

The youngest Cocoris daughter, Joanna Cocoris Hufham, contributed her own Bright Star history.

It sure was fun growing up with grandparents who were not only generous and kind, but restaurant owners to boot! I would always order a cheeseburger and french fries when we came to "The Store," as we call it . . . a little known fact is that the Bright Star makes the best cheeseburger. Then around age nine I tried fried snapper and then ate it exclusively for about six years straight! The employees were always so kind to us. Our pieces of pie were always the biggest . . . and if we said we wanted ice cream somehow it would magically appear even though I don't think it was on the menu. We drank Shirley Temples with extra cherries, and no one ever seemed to mind when we wanted to sit behind the register or hang out in the kitchen and watch.

I am the youngest of the three girls in our family, and the one who stirred up the most trouble. I have vivid memories of taking handfuls of chocolate crème de menthes and peppermint patties from behind the register and stuffing them into my pockets. My grandfather would just laugh, make me put some back, and then hand me an empty cigar box to store my loot.

I was very intrigued by a particular locked cabinet behind the register. Upon locating the key and sneaking a look I was extremely disappointed to find some very small bottles of something called "Jack Daniels." I feel sure that some of the Bright Star patrons were annoyed to find that many times their salt shakers contained sugar. And the employees from the telephone company next door were also irritated when their outdoor deposit slot was jammed full of slips reading "Guess Who?" on Monday mornings.

When I was in high school I worked on Sundays and on some of the busy holidays doing whatever was needed. Many times I gave out numbers to folks and was simply amazed and thankful that people would come and wait sometimes thirty to forty-five minutes in the hot sun or rain with their families.

When I worked behind the register my grandparents and uncles always said to be sure to ask if everyone had enjoyed their meal. Then afterward they would come ask for all the comments, positive and negative. They always wanted the best for the customers and to make sure that no one left hungry!

At that young age I was very enamored by the restaurant business; the servers, hostesses, and cashiers were all very glamorous to me. As an adult I realize of course the tireless efforts required to run a restaurant like the Bright Star. My family's hard work and sacrifices are the reason for this celebration.

I feel very blessed to have had grandparents who lived into my college years. When someone tells me, "Your grandparents were the kindest people," I can say, "Yes, I know they were." Our uncles are like second fathers to us. They have unconditionally supported all our endeavors . . . even when I wanted to go to coeducational camp! When I asked my husband, David, why he chose "The Store" to surprise me with an engagement ring he simply said, "Because it's like your home." And to quote my father-in-law, the late H. Paul Hufham, Jr., who was a big fan of the Bright Star and a dear friend of both uncles, "It's not just the food, it's the fellowship."

May Their Memory Be Eternal

The close of the 1980s saw a storied era come to an end at the Bright Star. On July 21, 1988, the family's beloved "Mr. Bill" passed away at age ninety-four. The heart that had reached out to so many people over the years finally came to rest. Never sick a day in his life, the patriarch of the family made the transition into the next life peacefully and gracefully. His penchant for a spoonful of olive oil and lemon juice every morning had served him well, providing him with good health and an active mind for almost a century.

Born in the Old World in 1894, Mr. Bill had traveled far and created a new home and a new life for almost seventy years in the New World. Always a regular at the Holy Trinity-Holy Cross Cathedral in Birmingham on Sunday mornings, until his later years, he also remained a familiar figure at the Bright Star Restaurant, visiting with patrons in the front booths until a couple of years before his death.

The *Birmingham Post-Herald* carried news of Bill Koikos's death on the front page. As well, Senator Richard Shelby paid tribute to his life in "An Outstanding Alabamian," which appeared in the *Congressional Record* of August 1, 1988. Pictures of Bill and Tasia Koikos hang in the restaurant today as a reminder of the legacy they have passed on to their family.

Never far from her husband during their fifty-two years together, Tasia succumbed to heart disease on March 25, 1989, just eight months after losing her beloved Bill. Together they had worked to raise themselves from the poverty of rural Greece to a prosperous life in Bessemer, Alabama. Their daughter, sons, and granddaughters were well established as Americans. These descendants would always remember their example of unceasing hard work, tempered with a strong sense of humor and an even stronger love for family—both the Koikos family and the Bright Star family.

The vital sense of hospitality that came so naturally to Bill and Tasia Koikos was described by an unknown historian, who wrote in August 2000, "They embodied the Greek notion of philotimo in which one's best efforts of food and fellowship are offered. It was the optimistic feeling that 'we will become friends—especially if we share food.'"

★8★

Approaching a Milestone

1990s–Present Day

We've seen a lot of restaurants come and go . . . but the Bright Star is still here.
—Marlon Tanksley

Closing Out the Century

The 1990s saw additional growth and further diversification of Bessemer's economic base. Though Trinity Industries closed its railcar manufacturing facility in 1997, a huge shot in the arm for the local economy came in 1993 when Mercedes-Benz located its only North American assembly plant in Vance, just minutes from Bessemer on I-20/59. Hundreds of new jobs were filled by a labor force of skilled workers, many of whom had received training at the Bessemer State Technical College and Lawson State Community College.

The Mercedes plant spawned numerous spin-off industries. Tier-one suppliers, such as German-based Oris Automotive Parts, planned an $8.5 million factory in Bessemer to supply the Mercedes M-Class vehicles being manufactured in Vance.

Exits at Academy Drive on Interstates 20/59 and at Morgan Road on I-459 have seen explosive growth in the retail, service, and hospitality sectors. Bessemer also began acquiring a reputation as a recreation destination. Visionland, the state's only water and theme park, was completed in 1998 and features numerous attractions. The facility, now known as Alabama Adventure, is under new business management that focuses on customer service and a growing marketing effort. Nearby Tannehill State Park offers excellent outdoor recreation. The area has also become a magnet for golfers with courses such as Tannehill National, Bent Brook, Oxmoor Valley, Frank House, and Ross Bridge.

New shopping opportunities began drawing people back to Bessemer. WaterMark Place Outlet Center led the way, followed by new retailers, such as United Textiles, in the historic downtown district.

During the waning days of the 1990s and the early days of the new millennium, the Bessemer Area Chamber of Commerce remained active in addressing the needs of the existing business community and continuing to promote the area to potential businesses. Ronnie Acker, the organization's president since 2001, cited the leadership of many of the area's businesspeople as cornerstones of their efforts to revitalize the city and the region. "Knowing the business leadership we have makes me the ultimate optimist about what is right about Bessemer and the western Jefferson County area," he stated.

"The leadership being shown by our businesspeople and community volunteers is uplifting, gratifying, positive, and exciting," Ronnie Acker wrote in What's Right about Bessemer in 2006. "Leaders like Vaughan Burrell (Long-Lewis), Timothy Thornton (UAB Medical West), Jerry Cherner (Jefferson Realty), Jordan Frazier (Jordan Frazier Chrysler Jeep Dodge), Faye Anderson (Manufacturing Packaging), Skipper Goodwin (First Financial), Hank Tyler (Henry H. Tyler Enterprises), Don Holmes (Holmes Oil), Joe Adams (ADCO), Joni Holt (Ken Holt Insurance), Dr. Raphael Weeks (Eagle Vision), Gene Cochran (Buffalo Rock), Anthony Underwood (Anthony Underwood Automotive), Pam Segars-Morris (Sebro Realty), Brian Hammonds (Brian's Carpet and Tile), Pam Nichols (Noland Health), Priscilla Dunn (State Representative), Colin Coyne (WaterMark Place), Howard Johnson (Holiday Bowl), [and] Charles Trammell (Bessemer YMCA) make the future look brighter and more positive."

The Industrial Development Board also continued its efforts to resculpt the crumbling downtown area. The board led the way in transforming the former Western Auto store into the Downtown Entrepreneurial Center, a business incubator with several start-up businesses. The city's Downtown Redevelopment Authority took control of several dilapidated buildings, and renovation began on a half block of Second Avenue and Nineteenth Street around the historic Berney Brothers Bank Building. Bessemer now has a National Historic District and an Urban Renewal District where construction code requirements for new buildings or renovations are enforced.

A New Venture

Life at the Bright Star in the 1990s was characterized by a continuation of the innovations that were put in place in the 1980s. The Taste of New Orleans weekends were as popular as ever; the Green Room and Dixie Room were proving an asset by drawing large parties to the restaurant; and the revitalization of downtown Bessemer and the surrounding area brought new people to the Bright Star.

Having been approached many times about opening a second restaurant, Jimmy and Nicky Koikos decided that the time was right to gamble on a new venture with their lifelong friend, Pete Gerontakis. The trio found another historic building, a white-pillared antebellum-style mansion on Birmingham's Southside, which was then home to the Pillars Restaurant. Tommy Finley came from the Bright Star to be general manager, and Chef Austin Davis came from Niki's Restaurant to implement a Creole-influenced menu focusing on the fresh seafood that the Koikos brothers were known for. They called the new restaurant the Merritt House in honor of the family that had originally lived there. From 1993 until 1999, diners enjoyed such dishes as turtle soup, snapper en papillote, and the Bright Star's own seafood gumbo for lunch and dinner. Though the restaurant was a success from the start, the partners sold the Merritt House in 1999 to a local restaurant group interested in opening a banquet business.

Carrot and Raisin Salad

This unusual side dish is especially popular on Mother's Day. Longtime Bright Star server Nita Ray Fitzgerald brought the recipe to the Bright Star from the Ensley Grill, where she worked in the 1960s.

5 pounds carrots, washed, peeled, and grated or finely chopped in food processor
1 1/2 cups mayonnaise
1 cup granulated sugar
1/2 cup shredded coconut
1 cup crushed pineapple
1 1/2 cups raisins

Place grated carrots in large mixing bowl. Add the remaining ingredients. Stir gently until thoroughly mixed. Refrigerate 2 hours or overnight.

Serves 10–12.

Tweaking the System

Back at the Bright Star, a new executive chef and general manager, Rick Daidone, arrived to replace James Veitch in 1990. He had been working at Jim 'n' Nick's barbeque restaurant and came to the Bright Star through his acquaintance with Tommy Finley. Rick set out to add new dishes to the menu like stuffed shrimp and a few of his own family's Italian-influenced recipes like veal parmesan. He also implemented a policy of offering a reduced menu on the Bright Star's busiest days. On Mother's Day, Valentine's Day, and Thanksgiving, patrons could choose from an abbreviated list of favorites, thus enabling the kitchen staff to keep up with crowds of up to 1,400 people.

In the tradition of the SAPS, the Breakfast Club convenes eighteen to twenty stalwarts every Saturday for convivial arguments, bacon and eggs, and the occasional round of pitching pennies or blackjack. The club formed around 1960, when Jimmy Koikos and friends Walter Pettey, Jim Creel, and Gus Gulas began meeting for breakfast once a week at Michael's on the Bessemer Super Highway, while Jimmy's father, Bill, minded the Bright Star. The club grew in number and eventually moved its gatherings to the Bright Star by the end of the 1960s.

The club, like the SAPS, revels in airing their various opinions on everything under the sun. They were waited on by the late Anne Mull for over twenty years, who as the only woman in the group matched them wisecrack for wisecrack. Now, Kathy Walden takes on the Breakfast Club, serving the meal at about 8 a.m., after the gentlemen have had an hour or so of coffee and chat.

Jim Holsumbake, a longtime friend of Jimmy and Nicky Koikos, commented that rarely does such a diverse group—businessmen, bankers, pipe shop workers, city employees, and truckers—come together for fellowship.

Rick Daidone and Nicky Koikos began attending the annual trade show held by the National Restaurant Association in Chicago. It was an opportunity to get new ideas for restaurant management and to see the latest in kitchen equipment, some of which found its way into the Bright Star's lineup. In 1997 the restaurant adopted a computer system to streamline the ordering process for the staff as well as to provide inventory and payroll information for the management.

Rick remained at the Bright Star until 2002. His brother, Ross, had by then joined the restaurant as kitchen manager.

Tide Tradition Continues

In the 1990s, Jimmy and Nicky continued their association with Alabama football through new friendships and patronage of the Bright Star by Bama alumni clubs.

Coach Gene Stallings and his family became regulars at the Bright Star soon after he became head coach at the University of Alabama in 1990. After Assistant Coach Jim Fuller first brought the Stallings family in to eat, Coach Stallings started dining at the Bright Star regularly and became friends with Jimmy Koikos. Such was the coach's partiality to the restaurant that Stallings's family, with Jimmy's collaboration, planned a surprise sixtieth-birthday party for him in the Green Room in 1995. Coach Stallings still calls the Bright Star one of his favorite restaurants, and he and Jimmy remain friends to this day. Jimmy has been a guest of Gene and Ruth Ann Stallings at their ranch in Texas.

University of Alabama alumni groups have used the

Bright Star as an unofficial clubhouse since the mid-1990s. The Red Elephant Club, which counts both Koikos brothers as members, is a booster club for Alabama football. Its members meet at the Bright Star once a month to hear speakers and for gridiron fellowship. The Tipoff Club serves a similar purpose for the Alabama basketball team. These organizations not only help maintain Jimmy and Nicky Koikos's connection to the University of Alabama, but they have also boosted weekday dinner business.

Day to Day: The Backbone of the Bright Star

Accommodating the volume of customers that the Bright Star serves on a daily basis requires an enormous amount of labor behind the scenes: ordering, receiving, and processing vast amounts of meat, seafood, and vegetables; broiling steaks and seafood in the time-honored Bright Star fashion; slow-cooking vegetables; preparing coffee and tea; turning dirty dishes into clean ones; and otherwise maintaining strict standards of cleanliness throughout the restaurant.

Several employees were interviewed for this book, and their comments are included as a valuable glimpse into the workings of the unique restaurant that they support. More important, these interviews give insight into the personalities behind the Bright Star "machine."

Ross Daidone has been employed at the Bright Star for thirteen years and has been the general manager for seven years. He remarked,

> It takes a lot of organization to get customers seated promptly, waited on, and served. That requires the staff getting here early and staying late. We're here from seven in the morning getting ready to open for lunch. Jimmy and I usually open, and Robert Moore is in the back prepping the kitchen. They're getting the food out for the cooks, cutting the meats, peeling potatoes, and they begin the slow-cooking process. The fish are delivered to us whole, and we begin cutting the fish early in the morning. We'll have vegetables delivered fresh five or six days a week. Fish is delivered three or four days weekly from the Gulf Coast. We have a special climate-controlled room where we cut the meat and fish.
>
> We try to keep the atmosphere in the kitchen light and upbeat, but we are very serious about getting our work done and getting food orders to our guests quickly and correctly.
>
> By 10:30, we're ready to open. Usually by 10:45, people are coming in for lunch. Jimmy is here by 7:00 a.m. on days when he opens, and by 10:30 on other days. He still washes the coffee urns like his daddy did years ago. Cleaning those urns has been a tradition here and a reason why our coffee tastes so good.

Betty Bailey has been a cook at the Bright Star since 1970.

It's a challenge to have a party of one hundred and you have to get all the food out to everybody at the same time. At times like that, everybody pitches in to help. On Sundays, we have to serve around nine hundred people in about three hours. That is a lot of work. But I remember Mr. Bill used to say that you should work as long as you feel good. He never missed a day while I was there. Always worked hard. Mr. Bill told me to drink a spoonful of olive oil and lemon juice every morning, like he did. And Miss Tasia made us aprons to wear. They were wonderful people.

Brenda Joyce "B. J." Salser has worked at the Bright Star for nineteen years, and has managed all the servers since the late 1990s. She offered these comments:

I work as a server, I handle reservations for banquets and parties, and I cashier. Pretty much anything that needs doing. I'm here six and sometimes seven days a week. And when I'm not here, they have my cell phone number and can reach me.

I enjoy the customers here more than anything. I know so many of them from having been here so long, and we have the most wonderful customers.

I've had a lot of memorable moments during my nineteen years. We've had wedding receptions and rehearsal dinners. People trust me to handle the decorations, the tables, the menu, and other items. I tell them to relax, enjoy themselves, and let us handle the details. And I've never had a single complaint.

Robert Moore, the daytime kitchen manager, has worked at the Bright Star for twenty-three years. He said of his daily routine at the Star,

We do our prep work the night before, and when we open at about seven we're ready to start cooking. We'll determine the number of vegetables by what we're serving for the entrees. We try to pair the vegetables with the meats and seafood dishes we're featuring that day. I'll do some of the cooking and I'll oversee the kitchen. We'll usually order around 2,500 pounds of fresh fish each week. We order whatever is the freshest; sometimes that's the snapper and sometimes it's grouper. Teamwork is the key to our operation. Everybody has to be on the same page for the kitchen to work efficiently.

Marie Jackson has been at the Bright Star for thirty-four years. She said, "I was working at another restaurant when I was told that the Bright Star was hiring. I came here and began fixing salads, then went to frying, and then to short order cook. Now I cook the vegetables. I'll get here in the morning and begin prepping the vegetables early. We'll usually have eight or nine vegetables on the menu each day."

Sonya Twitty is a server, bartender, and bar manager at the Bright Star. She stated,

> I wear a lot of hats here, and I enjoy each of them. I'll work five to six days a week bartending, serving, coordinating events, creating menus, hostessing, cashiering, whatever needs to be done. I have been here for twelve years, and I've met a lot of wonderful people here.
>
> You have to be able to get along and work well together to stay in this business. Sometimes during the holiday season I'll see the staff here more than I see my family. I really enjoy working with everyone here. We're a family.
>
> A special memory for me is one night when we had a party of 100 scheduled on the wrong night. I was on my way home when the mistake was realized and they phoned me. I did a U-turn in the middle of the street, called my husband and told him to fix something for the kids, and headed back to the Bright Star. We called some of our folks and got them out of the shower, but everybody came back to pitch in. And everything went off without a hitch.
>
> We're very blessed to have such a wonderful relationship with our staff and our customers. We have the best customers in the world.

Spinach and Rice Casserole

When Marie Jackson prepares this casserole for lunch, there is a standing list of Bright Star customers who want to know about it—via phone or fax machine!

3 10-ounce packages frozen chopped spinach, thawed and squeezed thoroughly

1/2 cup chopped green onions
1 cup cooked white rice
1 egg, slightly beaten
1/4 cup crumbled feta cheese
1/2 cup Parmesan cheese

Preheat oven to 350°. Butter a 9 x 13 baking dish generously. In a bowl, thoroughly mix together all ingredients. Put in baking dish.

For topping:

2 1/2 cups milk
1 chicken bouillon cube
1/2 cup butter (1 stick), melted
1/4 cup all-purpose flour

Heat milk and simmer (do not boil). Add bouillon cube to hot milk and stir until dissolved. Set aside. In a bowl, blend melted butter and flour together, then slowly into heated milk and mix well. Pour topping over spinach mixture. Bake at 350° for 20 minutes or until golden brown.

Serves 8–10.

Marlon Tanksley is maitre d' at the Bright Star. He has been at the Bright Star for twenty-eight years.

I especially enjoy Mother's Day, our biggest day of the year. Working with Jamie Shannon at our Taste of New Orleans nights was great, too.

The biggest change I've seen here over the years is the [2001] expansion that gave us the lounge and the waiting area. The area is comfortable and it gives me an opportunity to meet and visit with our customers who are waiting to be seated.

I thank God for my health and hope I can continue working here for a long time. We've seen a lot of restaurants come and go in the area, but the Bright Star is still here.

Carl Thomas has been at the Bright Star since 1975.

We have fun here, but we get our work done. Mr. Jimmy put it in our heads that we have to give 110 percent. One hundred is not good enough. There was a lot of competition out there and we had to give 110 percent to stay on top.

Mr. Bill once told me that Jimmy and Nicky both liked me and the work I was doing. He told me that I'll do great things here. And we are doing great things at the Bright Star. I couldn't be doing anything else. I thought at first I'd be here for a short while and then go on to something else. Now I know I'm doing what I'm supposed to be doing. I thank God for that.

We started out striving to be the best and we are. Sometimes we're serving 800 or 900 people on a busy day. I don't know of another restaurant that can put out that much food so quickly and correctly.

Walter Hoskins has been employed at the Bright Star since 1967. "I enjoy working here because of the fairness of it," he said. "Improvements are made constantly, particularly in equipment, salad bar, in the way the business is run, and they make it a good place to work."

A final story from server Jeff Golson illustrates what unexpected things can happen during day-to-day business. "One day a middle-aged lady and her two young adult children came in for dinner carrying an urn filled with their grandmother's ashes," he remembered. "Granny's last wish was to have her final dinner at the Bright Star. They sat down in a booth, where Granny had her own place complete with her picture, urn, and a candle burning alongside."

Wedding Bells

As Jimmy and Nicky intended, the Green and Dixie rooms have been used for private, large groups since they were added in the late 1980s. John G. Cocoris, their brother-in-law, was surprised with a sixtieth-birthday party in the Green Room in 1992, and nearly all of the Cocoris grandchildren have had baptism celebrations there.

Two customers wrote to share wedding stories involving the Bright Star. Amy Holland of Cullman, Alabama, wrote,

> The Bright Star holds a very special place in my and my husband's hearts. In mid-November 1993, my husband, Kevin, and I decided to have dinner at the Bright Star to celebrate our two years of dating. Kevin had recently accepted a job in Mobile, Alabama, and would be moving shortly. We had a lot to discuss and celebrate that evening.
>
> I opened my anniversary gift from Kevin (the Christmas advent calendar that I had asked for), and as I was looking at each detailed handmade ornament in its own individual pocket I came to the eleventh day and attached to a green ribbon was a gorgeous engagement ring. At that moment he asked me to marry him. Of course I said yes and then I cried as he put the ring on my finger. I remember one of the owners of the Bright Star coming by to congratulate us as did several of the personnel. After a fabulous rehearsal dinner at the Bright Star the evening of March 10, 1995, Kevin and I were married on Saturday, March 11, 1995, at our then hometown church, Pleasant Ridge Baptist in Hueytown.
>
> Now almost eleven years and two kids later (Caroline, age seven, and Grant, age three) we decided to come back to the Bright Star for our tenth anniversary. Of course the food was as fabulous as it has always been. . . .
>
> The Bright Star is a spectacular restaurant and we plan on dining there for years to come.

More wedding-related memories came from Sherry and Denney Owen.

> Our daughter and her husband (Leigh and Drew Bardenwerper) were married at the Bright Star Restaurant on August 19, 2005. One of their first dates was there, and they fell in love with the elegance of the restaurant. They both wanted a memorable, cozy, sit-down dinner wedding and immediately thought of the Bright Star. The atmosphere, food, and service were absolutely perfect. Many guests told

us of their fond memories of eating at the restaurant in the past. Others told us that they had heard of the historic restaurant and were anxious to attend the wedding.

Brenda Salser made planning the wedding stress free. She and her professional staff accommodated us in every way.

Leigh and Drew have dined at the Bright Star several times since they married and plan to celebrate their first and many more anniversaries at your wonderful restaurant.

Shelter from the Sun

For decades, customers had become accustomed to waiting in long lines outdoors, whatever the weather, to get into the Bright Star on their busiest days. The Koikos brothers saw an opportunity to improve this situation in early 2001, when Jay-Mark Jewelers, a longtime tenant of the corner space in the Realty Building, closed its doors. Jimmy and Nicky decided to take over that space to create a substantial waiting room and bar area for the comfort and convenience of their clientele.

Architect Vic Fortinberry designed a new entrance on the corner of Third Avenue and Nineteenth Street that opened into a long, sunlit waiting room with a tiled floor and built-in benches and planters. Nicky Koikos realized that his new waiting room needed a focal point, so he commissioned artist Anita Bice to paint a mural on the wall leading into the main dining room from the new waiting room. She depicted the 1907, 1911, and 1913 locations of the Bright Star as well as historic sites in the city, county, and state. Nicky said, "It was interesting to see Anita work her magic as the blank wall became a beautiful mural." Bice also restored photographs of all of the Bright Star's owners over the years to create a portrait gallery inside the new entrance.

The darker, more intimate bar area, with plenty of television sets for sports lovers, offered shelf space that allowed the Bright Star to provide a larger variety of premium wines and top-shelf liquors. Two restrooms were added conveniently near the new entrance. The former entrance, which had served as the main public access since 1915, was converted into an exit only. The waiting area that had been added alongside the Green and Dixie rooms became the Anastasia Room, named after Tasia Koikos.

Construction began with C. N. Bailey as general contractor in April 2001 and was completed in September with a ribbon-cutting ceremony.

The Heart and Soul of the Bright Star

Since the 1960s, Jimmy and Nicky have been a constant presence at the Bright Star Restaurant. Their dedication to the business and their hands-on management style has created a tremendously loyal work-

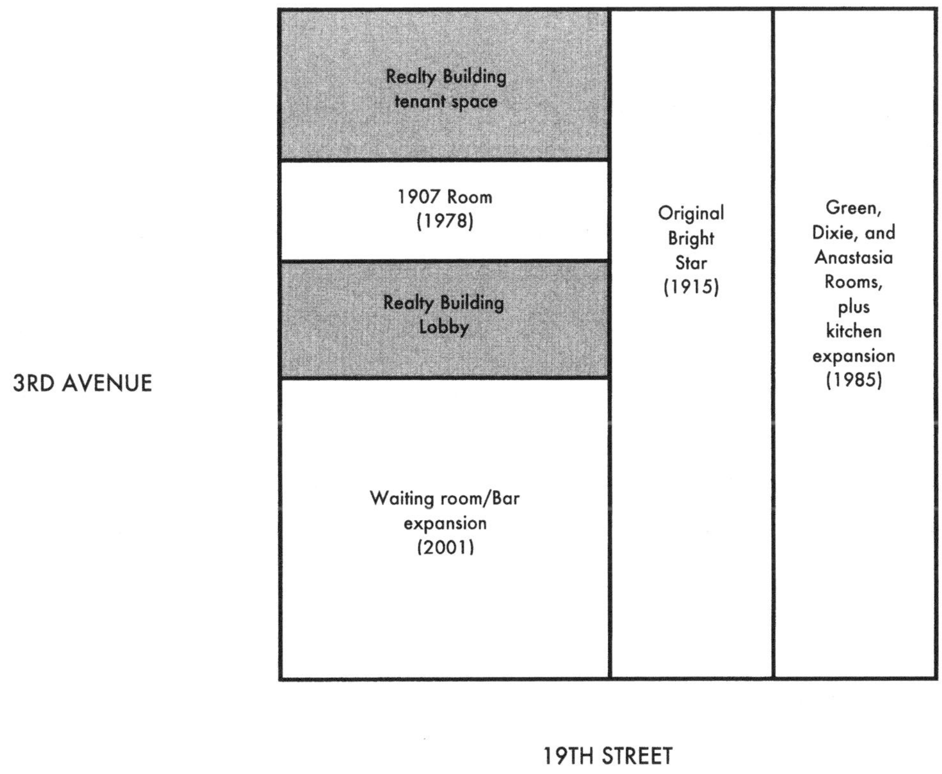

Diagrammatic floor plan of the current Bright Star showing its various expansions. (Courtesy of Connie Cocoris Chwe.)

force. Remarkably, approximately 35 percent of this workforce (twenty-eight out of eighty employees) have worked at the restaurant for ten years or longer.

Sonya Twitty, current bar manager, commented on the work ethic of Jimmy and Nicky. "Jimmy and Nicky are two of the hardest-working restaurant owners I've ever known," she said. "They are extremely hands-on and handle every detail personally. I've worked for other restaurants, and I respect Jimmy and Nicky more than any other employer I've had. It's an honor to work for them, and I plan on retiring here."

Cooks, porters, expediters, cashiers, and waitstaff enjoy working for Jimmy and Nicky because of the culture they have created that emphasizes loyalty between employee and employer, strong communication, and appreciation for a job well done.

The cumulative effect of the Bright Star's remodelings and expansions since 1966 and the renewed commercial activity in the Bessemer area is a customer volume that astonishes outsiders. According to General Manager Ross Daidone, the restaurant feeds approximately 400 people during lunch on a weekday. Dinners during the week see around 150 customers, while on Friday and Saturday nights that number increases to between 350 and 400 people.

Sunday lunch remains a regular event, with around 800 people sitting down between 11:00 and 3:00. On Mother's Day, typically the busiest day of the year, approximately 1,400 people are served in five and a half hours. An additional 300 diners are served that evening.

The Bright Star is open on Thanksgiving Day and typically serves 1,500 people between 10:00 and 5:00. In addition, the restaurant serves over 500 people on Valentine's Day for dinner, and over 500 people on New Year's Eve. It is interesting to note that take-out meals account for about 10 percent of these sales. The Bright Star also sells its delicious homemade pies.

Betty Bailey, a chef who has worked at the Bright Star for thirty-seven years, remarked on what the Koikoses mean to her. "Jimmy and Nicky and the family helped raise my children. They've helped me a lot over the years. We worked hard, and we knew that the family was loyal to us. They would do anything to help their employees. Jimmy and I never had a cross word in thirty-seven years. Now, Nicky and I got into it once, but we both apologized and have been best friends ever since."

Current executive chef Austin Davis also praised Jimmy and Nicky's empathic management style: "Jimmy and Nicky both have the personal touch. They take care of problems. You can sit down and talk over your personal problems and they will listen. I feel like I am family because of the way I am treated and respected, and in turn I give respect. Everyone cares about each other. That is why I stay. I feel good about coming to work. I am blessed. I am happy. I plan to retire here."

Roy Moore, a chef and brother of Chef Robert Moore, commented on his experiences with Jimmy and Nicky.

I feel that Jimmy and Nicky are good friends. They gave me my first job. One day Nicky was sitting at a booth with his back to me, but I could not see him. One of the other porters told me I had to move a bunch of trash boxes that were stacked up by the front door. I said, "What are you talking about, I am not going to move those boxes!" Nicky looked around and said, "Who said that?" I raised my hand and he started to laugh and said that he respected an honest man. He said,

"I'll get someone to help you with that." I knew from then on, I would enjoy working at the restaurant.

Both owners know how to maintain their equipment and dining rooms. They also appreciate you so much. One time Jimmy called and asked me to come in unexpectedly. I dropped my plans and came in. Jimmy said, "Thank you, you really showed you are a Bright Star man, and I appreciate that."

Robert Moore echoed his brother's comments. "Jimmy and Nicky always compliment us on a job well done," he said. "Sometimes after a really big night they'll post a note in the kitchen thanking us for all we did. It lets us know that we're doing something right."

Another key to the continued success of the Bright Star is the contrasting yet complementary styles of Jimmy and Nicky. The employees appreciate what each man contributes to the collective success of the restaurant. As Chef Austin Davis put it, "You can't ask for a better family-owned restaurant. Nicky is the back-of-the-house man; Jimmy, the front-of-the-house man. They meet in the middle of the house and collaborate. It is the best—you have to experience it."

Ross Daidone reflected on the differing management style of Jimmy and Nicky.

> Jimmy is the best front man in the business. I've worked at other restaurants, and I've never seen anyone handle the front of a restaurant better than Jimmy. He has a natural ability for public relations and for greeting people.
>
> Nicky's talent has always been coordinating the kitchen activities. He's amazing at keeping everything running and knowing exactly what is going on throughout the restaurant. Sometimes he's even taking orders and working in the kitchen as an expediter. He assists the servers in getting their orders in and getting the food to the guests promptly.

Server Brenda Adams recollected her experiences with Jimmy and Nicky: "I have the highest respect for Jimmy. He means business. If he sees an empty coffee cup, he will tell you immediately. He believes in giving guests a refill and is very strict about guest service. He is interested in your making a good tip and will help you out any way he can. Nicky is always available to help in the kitchen and will help you if you get behind in your orders. His main concern is the kitchen." Margaret Dunkin added, "Nicky is a joy to work with. When we are slammed, he is a breath of fresh air. When he sees a need he just jumps in and helps. He makes sure the guests don't have to wait any longer than they have to. He helps everybody."

The accolades of their staff testify to the success of Jimmy and Nicky's inclusive and empathic management style. As veteran server Nancy Whittington summed it up, "They are very much to be admired. Two brothers who work together all of these years side by side. They love each other. They are loyal and dedicated."

Bright Star across the Nation

Over the course of its century of service to the people of Bessemer, the Bright Star Restaurant has been spotlighted on the local, regional, and national stages. Among the honors the restaurant has garnered was being named one of the nation's best neighborhood restaurants by *Bon Appétit* magazine in 2003.

Countless articles in publications such as *Southern Living, Portico,* and *Tuscaloosa* magazines, the *Birmingham News,* the *Western Star,* and the *Birmingham Post-Herald* have featured the restaurant's outstanding food, the unique employment longevity of its staff, and the immigrant family that launched the business one hundred years ago.

The Bright Star has thrice been entered into the Congressional Record of the United States. Representative (now Senator) Richard Shelby honored "Mr. Bill" Koikos from the floor of the U.S. House of Representatives in March 1980 and again after his death in 1988. Senator Howell Heflin paid tribute to the restaurant and its employees in a speech to the Senate on September 27, 1995.

Several customer anecdotes verify that the Bright Star's reputation has reached far beyond the Bessemer city limits and that it is the benchmark against which other restaurants are measured. Longtime customer Betty Campbell recounted, "My husband and I used to travel a lot, and I remember we had just arrived in Los Angeles on a flight from Hong Kong. The pilot was greeting us as we were getting off the plane and asked where we were from. We told him that we were from a small town called Bessemer just outside Birmingham. 'Oh,' he said, 'that's the place that has the Bright Star Restaurant!' We also met some people in Chicago who knew of the Bright Star. It seems that people know the Bright Star everywhere we've been. We've eaten at many fine restaurants around the world, but we've never had a better meal than those we've enjoyed at the Bright Star."

Will Simmons began coming to the Bright Star when he was about nine years old, accompanying his father, who made deliveries to the restaurant every Saturday morning for Home Baking Company. "I've eaten at restaurants in London, Barcelona, Nice, Monte Carlo, Rome, Malaga, Turkey, Athens, Venice, and other places," he said. "They all had good food, but I was always glad to get back to the Bright Star. Once, I brought one of [the Bright Star's] pies with me to Pennsylvania. I had it on the plane and the stewardesses wanted me to share with them. I gave each of them a small piece."

Ronnie Acker, president of the Bessemer Area Chamber of Commerce, added, "The restaurant shares a parking lot with the chamber, and I often walk to lunch here. I notice the license plates of cars from all over Alabama who come here to eat. Bessemer has always been close to my heart, and the Bright Star is the heart of Bessemer."

Vicki and Jim Briley have been coming to the Bright Star together throughout their twenty-eight years of marriage. "The Bright Star is a unique place with a special atmosphere," they remarked. "All these years and the Bright Star has never disappointed us a single time. Once, while we were looking for a place to eat in San Francisco, we were asking ourselves, 'Wonder where their Bright Star is?' We've always felt that if the Bright Star ever closed, it would be like turning out the lights in Bessemer."

Longtime customer Melinda Miles remarked, "I live in Tampa, Florida, now and come to the Bright Star when I'm in town visiting relatives. As a matter of fact, I'm leaving right now to return to Tampa, and I have a pie to go that I'm taking with me! How about that, a whole pineapple-cheese pie that's going all the way to Florida!" Mary Sue Griffin, a high school friend of Helen Cocoris, remembered "always going to the Bright Star during our summer visits from California many times and [flying] back to California with three children and two quarts of gumbo!"

Devoted fan Ennis Byrdsong sent these comments from up North: "I live in Michigan and I visit [the Bright Star] three or four times per year. As soon as I get off of the airplane, my first order of business is to eat at your restaurant. . . . I have been to a lot of places and I have eaten at a lot of restaurants, but no one's food even comes close to yours. I brag about your food to my friends in Michigan."

Similarly, Mr. and Mrs. Mitchell Ede of Cincinnati wrote, "On our yearly visit to Mr. and Mrs. Murray Armstrong of Trussville, Alabama, we look forward to dining at your wonderful restaurant. We appreciate your superior food, outstanding service, and overall Southern hospitality. It is unusual to find such a gem in a small town."

Brenda Kathryn Hathcock Hastings grew up in Bessemer but moved away after graduation from high school. She wrote, "So many years have gone by; I have lived in many places over these decades—Nashville, Ft. Lauderdale, Charleston, Pensacola, Cincinnati, Indianapolis, Orlando, and I have now just recently moved back to Alabama, near Mobile. . . . Of all the cities in which I have lived and traveled and their many restaurants, the Bright Star is still the best."

Next Up . . .

Stacey Cocoris Craig, the oldest of Helen Koikos Cocoris's three daughters, has a part-time job at the

Bright Star today. She joined the management team in 2001 after ten years as a corporate lender. Her duties include marketing, financial analysis, general accounting, and management of the Realty Building's tenants.

Stacey has been able to market the Bright Star in new ways, including building a Bright Star web site and organizing a birthday club, whose members receive discount coupons for their birthday month. She has compiled an e-mail database of over six thousand customer names for use in her marketing programs.

These accomplishments as well as other plans are the natural result of Stacey's upbringing in and around the Bright Star. She states,

> Uncle Jim and Uncle Nick had a big presence during our childhood. Uncle Jim is the charismatic front man and makes you feel really welcome as you walk in the door. Nicky is the conscientious manager who cares deeply about the restaurant, its guests, and its employees.
>
> Through their hard work and discipline the restaurant has tripled in size over the last forty years and has earned a statewide following. They deserve all the credit for assembling a terrific staff and consistently creating an excellent dining experience. I hope to continue my involvement in the Bright Star restaurant for many years in the future.

Nicky and Jimmy Koikos with niece Stacey Cocoris on the eve of her wedding to Hugh B. Craig IV, February 23, 2001. (Courtesy of the Koikos family.)

As the Bright Star Restaurant reaches the milestone of its one-hundredth anniversary, Jimmy and Nicky Koikos are proud of its tradition of serving delicious steaks, seafood, and vegetables in an environment where guests are treated as family. Though a second location has been discussed many times, the brothers believe the Bright Star experience is not easily duplicated, and so they will continue to focus their efforts on maintaining and improving the famous Bright Star consistency in food and service.

The brothers realize much of the success of the Bright Star is due to the loyalty and hard work of its staff, whom they deeply appreciate. Jimmy and Nicky have always managed their employees according to this philosophy: "It is important to treat your employees as you want them to treat your best guests." The success of the philosophy is evident in the guest letters in chapter 11.

As the restaurant enters its second century, Jimmy Koikos still relishes his role as maitre d' and "front man" and is as motivated as ever. As Jimmy noted, "The restaurant business is the best business in the world. I have met an extraordinary number of good people over the years. Our guests show a lot of respect for the restaurant, and it has been a real pleasure to watch generations of families eat at the Bright Star." Nicky Koikos remains the quiet force overseeing food preparation and service. He echoed his brother's appreciation: "These days our patrons have many dining options available to them, particularly with the growth of the chain restaurants. The Bright Star has a unique atmosphere, and I believe our guests feel right at home. I want to thank our guests sincerely for their patronage over the years."

(Courtesy of Bob Farley.)

(Courtesy of Bob Farley.)

★9★

The Bright Star Hall of Fame

The Bright Star Hall of Fame

A restaurant that remains in business for one hundred years has obviously cultivated a talented and loyal staff both in the dining room and in the kitchen. The Koikos brothers rely on their employees to take care of customers with the attention to detail that has been a Bright Star hallmark since it opened in 1907. Whether planning a wedding reception, turning out a flawless dinner for one hundred people, or simply keeping the iced tea and coffee replenished, the managers, chefs, and waitstaff display an attitude of genuine caring and friendliness that is as important as the delicious food.

Jimmy and Nicky Koikos are also proud that a significant percentage of their employees stay at the Bright Star for many years. This is a result of the feeling of family that pervades the restaurant's atmosphere. In addition, four mother-daughter teams have worked as servers at the Bright Star: Nita Ray and Judy Ray; Bessie Lloyd and Lucy Schultz; Luverne Jordan and Sherry Parsons; and Brenda Adams and Tammy Adams Golson.

Following is a list of current Bright Star employees who have been with the restaurant for ten years or more. This list represents approximately 35 percent of the total number of people employed at the Bright Star.

JIMMY'S RIGHT-HAND MAN

Stacey Cocoris Craig offered this tribute to maitre d' Marlon Tanksley, whose career at the Bright Star exemplifies their standard of customer service.

I have had the pleasure of working with Marlon Tanksley at the Bright Star since 1979, when we were both fourteen years old. A graduate of Abrams High School, Marlon began his career as a porter and then worked as a dishwasher and expediter before training under Jimmy as a host. His quiet, pleasant personality, strong work ethic (he often works seven days a week), and amazing skill in seating reservations caught Jimmy's eye. Upon the departure of Nick Costas in 1995, Marlon was promoted to the post of maitre d', where he has remained ever since.

Marlon's time outside the Bright Star is spent with his family. He and his wife, Michelle, have two daughters, Wykeria and Ashanta.

It is not an understatement to say that the Bright Star would never be able to operate with its legendary speed and volume without Marlon's gifts. His ability to handle reservations and walk-in guests in a friendly, calm manner is as remarkable as his speed in setting up tables. I have learned so much about how to manage guest relations from him since I began working at the Bright Star on a full-time basis in 2001. He is simply the best in the business.

As Jimmy noted, "Marlon is a very respected gentleman at the Bright Star restaurant. People know and love him. He sees people and knows where they want to sit sometimes better than I do. His sharp mind, bright smile, and talent for placing guests are some of the keys to the continued success of the Bright Star Restaurant."

Name ★ Starting Date

Walter Hoskins ★ 1967
Betty Bailey ★ 1970
Marie Jackson ★ 1974
Carl Thomas ★ 1975
Marlon Tanksley ★ 1979
Felisa "Ann" Tolbert ★ 1979
Brenda Adams ★ 1983
Rita Weems ★ 1983
Robert Moore ★ 1984
Wanda Little ★ 1984
Sarah Marshall ★ 1986
George "Tony" Feagins ★ 1988
Linda Jarrett ★ 1988
Evelyn Rembert ★ 1988
Brenda Salser ★ 1988
Neda Arthur ★ 1990
Jeff Golson ★ 1990
Jean Smith ★ 1993
James Boone ★ 1994
Ross Daidone ★ 1994
Austin Davis ★ 1994
Jimmie Turner ★ 1994
Nancy Whittington ★ 1994
Sonya Twitty ★ 1994
Mary "Kathy" Walden ★ 1994
Margaret Dunkin ★ 1996
Keith McClendon ★ 1997
Roy Moore ★ 1997

Current Bright Star employees are pictured on following page.

Bright Star maitre d' Marlon Tanksley, 2006. (Courtesy of the Koikos family.)

Bright Star employees, all with ten or more years of service, March 9, 2007. *Seated* (left to right): Wanda Little, cook; Bettie Bailey, cook; Neda Arthur, server; Ann Tolbert, cook; and Evelyn Rembert, cook. *Front row* (standing, left to right): Linda Jarrett, server; Kathy Walden, server; Jean Smith, server; Rita Weems, server; Lee Williams, server; Sarah Marshall, cook; Brenda Salser, head server; Sonya Twitty, bar and beverage manager; and Marie Jackson, cook. *Back row* (standing, left to right): Tony Feagins, executive chef; Austin Davis, executive chef; Nancy Whittington, server; Robert Moore, executive chef; Ross Daidone, general manager; and Keith McClendon, porter. (Courtesy of the Koikos family.)

★10★

Our Fallen Stars

The Bright Star family would like to lovingly acknowledge the following employees who passed away during or since their years at the Bright Star. All of these fine people, in their various roles at the restaurant, made an indelible impression on those whom they knew during their time at the Bright Star.

Gwen Atkinson

Durone Boles

Pat Creel

Tammy Adams Golson

Cliff Isom

Carrie Lee LeFurgey

Bessie Lloyd

Anne Mull

Irene Pickens

Mary Helen Warren

Fannie Wrigh

Bright Star server Mary Helen Warren with Miss America 1995, Heather Whitestone. (Courtesy of Diane Parks.)

Anne Mull was a server at the Bright Star from 1980 until her death in March 2005. Over the years, her devotion to the restaurant led to responsibilities beyond the scope of her job description. For example, Anne often opened the restaurant in Jimmy Koikos's stead for chefs and vendors and helped manage reservations of large groups. She came to understand the Bright Star's operations nearly as well as the owners themselves, and they both valued her feedback on guest and employee issues. The exceptional strength of her work ethic is shown simply by the fact that after her death, the Bright Star had to hire three employees to replace her.

A tall, slim redhead, Anne's wry sense of humor endeared her to coworkers and to her loyal customers as much as her unflagging professionalism did. This mistress of the witty rejoinder was a natural choice to work with the Breakfast Club, which still meets on Saturday mornings at the restaurant. "Anything that the men thought up, Anne gave back to them with an extra punch," said Jimmy Koikos. Evidence of Anne's sparkling personality is seen in chapter 11, where she is mentioned by many customers who wrote letters to the Bright Star.

In memory of this beloved Bright Star figure, who requested that she be buried wearing her server's uniform, the following stories are offered. Server Rita Weems shared three memories of her coworker.

Anne was serving a table and was in the process of reciting the pies we had for dessert. After she had rattled them off, the guest said, "I bet you can't do that backward." Anne said, "Oh yes I can!"—and proceeded to turn around to recite them again with her back facing the guests.

Another time Anne was asked, "Do you have crab legs?" She looked down, lifted her pants leg, rubbed her leg back and forth, and said, "No, sir, not the last time I checked!"

Then there once was a guest who had had the hiccups for two days straight and said that he could not get rid of them. (It was not Anne's guest.) Anne went straight up to him and said, "Sir, did you know that you are the father of my firstborn child?" The man did not know Anne and was about to choke, but it cured his hiccups!

Server Paula Christian recalled, "Anne had just set a tray of food down in the Anastasia Room. As she was walking away, one of the customers at her table exclaimed, 'Oh, God, I wanted French fries instead of a baked potato!' Without missing a beat, Anne turned back and replied, 'Sorry, dear, I'm only God on Thursdays.'"

The last word comes from customers Lane Gibbs and Fred Blevins, who, as part of the "Kiss My Grits" gang, constituted some of Anne's loyal following. They wrote, "We always requested Anne 'Flo' Mull. We tried to get the best of her, but she always got the upper hand. We sure do miss her."

Just like the rest of her family at the Bright Star.

★ 11 ★

In Their Own Words

Letters and Interviews from Our Customers

Letters and Interviews from Our Customers

To Jimmy and Nicky Koikos, the greatest tribute that can be paid to the business that members of their family began a century ago is praise from their loyal customers. Many of those customers have frequented the restaurant for forty and even fifty years, traveling from throughout Alabama to enjoy the culinary excellence they have come to expect from the Bright Star.

Over the course of its century of service to the people of Bessemer, Jefferson County, and the state of Alabama, the Bright Star has touched countless lives. The restaurant that began as the dream of an immigrant family has itself become "family" to thousands who have helped it become a Bessemer landmark. When the Koikos, Cocoris, Chwe, Craig, and Hufham families decided to commemorate the one-hundredth anniversary of the founding of the Bright Star, they wanted to include in the volume personal stories about and memories of the restaurant. They appealed to friends, former and current staff, and loyal patrons for help in collecting these accounts.

The response was overwhelming. Detailed letters, e-mails, and handwritten notes came in from the Birmingham area and across the country. They told poignant stories of special memories that these customers, many of whom had become dear friends, held of the Bright Star and the people who lovingly operated the restaurant. In addition, some customers consented to be interviewed, and their words are transcribed here.

The memories include times of joy and times of sorrow. Of a young man on his knees placing an engagement ring on the finger of the girl he had just asked to be his bride. Of families gathering in a quiet booth to honor the memory of their beloved mother. Of a young man and woman celebrating a meal together before he would ship off to war. Of couples whose lives took them far from the Bessemer neighborhoods of their youth but where they always return to find the restaurant they had known as children. Of youngsters beaming at being handed a treasure from Mr. Bill's candy jar.

It is a custom and unwritten rule at the Bright Star for customers to be treated as if they are family. In fact, they are family. As in any family, the owners of the Bright Star and their patrons from Bessemer and throughout Alabama who have made the restaurant the success it is today shared good times as well as hard times together.

Philoxenia is a Greek word meaning "friend of a stranger." In Greece, it is more than a word; it is a way of life. It dictates the way visitors are received into a home in that country. It was the founding philosophy of Tom Bonduris when he opened his restaurant in 1907. It remained the focus of the families who followed him and is the ultimate goal of the people who continue to welcome customers to the Bright Star today.

It is with great thanks to those who contributed these stories that the Bright Star family presents these letters, largely unedited, as part of this work.

Letters

As I recall, there was once a well-known men's club that met at the Bright Star every Saturday morning. This is the story as I heard it. The menu consisted of bacon, eggs, pancakes, etc., and very good coffee. The coffee was strong but you could also order stronger liquids to suit your appetite. Whatever the fare, all the men left with a smile on their faces and seemed very happy. Happy hour came early in those days.

Another memory I have is that of my girls. When they were babies we went for our Friday night dinner, and they would be in highchairs with crackers to munch. The youngest remembers the wonderful shrimp she ate there, especially recalls that cute dish with the ice around it to cool the shrimp. She still loves shrimp and knows the Bright Star is the best place to eat.

And the most honest folks own it. The owner called my husband very late one night and said he had overpaid, so please mention this the next time he came in.

Mrs. Ralph Towers

My memories of the Bright Star go back to when I was around ten years old, which was forty years ago. I remember my father, the late Tony B. Cacioppo, Sr., would take my family to the Bright Star every Friday night. If we didn't eat at the restaurant, we ordered take-out. Our favorite dish was none other than fried snapper, fries, and salad with Thousand Island dressing. I remember my sister, Josephine, and I shared a plate for a while but then our parents realized that we could finish a plate on our own with no trouble.

Another memory I cherish is when my cousins and some friends before Christmas would write our names on a piece of paper and put them in a hat. We each took turns drawing out the names. On a Saturday morning, we would get one of our parents to drive us to downtown Bessemer to shop at Kress or McClellan's department stores to buy a gift or toy for the person we drew. We had a limit of $2 to spend. This was around 1966.

When we finished shopping, we would go to the Bright Star to eat lunch. A waitress would look at all of us kids and say, "Follow me," and take us past the kitchen to a booth with drawn curtains. There must've been around twelve kids, eight to twelve years of age. You should've seen the looks on all the customers' faces when we walked in with no adult supervision. Everyone handled themselves with dignity, which is more than I can say of today's children. We ordered our meals and then exchanged gifts. When it came time to pay our bills, I remember my older cousins asking one person at a time, "How much money do you have?" Somebody would say $1.75, another would say $1.25, and another would say 85 cents. Finally, we got up enough to pay our bills.

There at the register was Mr. Bill Koikos, Jimmy and Nick's father. Everyone that's been to the Bright Star knows there's a bowl of peppermint patties on the counter. This was some of my cousins' first time eating there and they were told that the restaurant gives away free candy after your meal and that Mr. Bill would ask, "You want a mint? You want a mint? A mint?" in his heavy Greek accent.

Mr. Bill thanked us children for our business and saw some of the kids staring at the bowl full of peppermint patties. They were just waiting for those famous words to come out of Mr. Bill's mouth. When he finally realized what we were waiting on, he said, "You kids want a mint? A mint? Take a mint." You thought thousand-dollar bills were being handed out. All these hands dug into the bowl and took every one of those peppermint patties, with Mr. Bill's approval.

Ah, the good old days. Congratulations, Bright Star, on your one-hundredth anniversary in 2007. I plan on visiting with my wife, Judy, and family for dinner.

Tony B. Cacioppo

In 1951, I worked at Bradley Grain and Grocery Company, which was a wholesale store on Fourth Avenue and Twentieth Street in Bessemer. On the last night of every month after the store closed, we took inventory. Before beginning our work, Mr. Bruce Bradley would take us all to dinner at the Bright Star. There would be ten to fifteen of us walking to the Bright Star. Lots of people were on the sidewalks after hours back then.

Mr. Bill and Mr. Pete would greet the customers, like Jimmy and Nicky do now. The most popular entrees on the menu were lamb chops and veal cutlets. I'm sure that they served steaks and oysters, but other seafoods were not as prevalent. The only dessert that I remember was toasted pound cake with a scoop of ice cream, which is very good and I still prepare it sometimes.

In 1959 I married Ben "Buzz" Vines, a bailiff in Judge Gardner Goodwyn's court. Juries were kept sequestered together much of the time back then, for sometimes more than a week, and my husband had to stay with them. The Bright Star was open for breakfast, lunch, and dinner, so sometimes jurors would eat three meals a day there for several days.

Oftentimes during a long trial, Mr. Bill would invite me to come to the Bright Star and eat the evening meal with Ben. These are very pleasant memories.

Ethel Parsons Vines

I am pleased to be a resident of Bessemer. One of the major reasons is that it is the site of the Bright Star Restaurant. The excellence in service, quality of delicious food, and attractive setting are what a diner enjoys when having a meal at the Bright Star. These are the outstanding principles which the family required when it was founded in 1907.

Congratulations to Jimmy and Nick on maintaining the traditional manner and prestige the Bright Star continues to enjoy through their operation.

Lila Davis

A few weeks ago, my husband and I were eating in your restaurant and we mentioned that the wall canvases were painted in my great-grandfather's store. You asked if we knew any history. My father wrote the following, based on the reminiscences of my grandmother, Sidney Morton Montgomery.

Fleta Edwards

Ninety years or so ago a traveling artist was hired by the café to decorate their wall with paintings. He was from Germany, so the scenes he painted are imaginary view of his country. That's a little odd, because the owners were originally from Greece and the menu almost a century later still has many Greek dishes. Rather than have the artist paint while the diners are eating, they looked for a place he could paint and then bring the canvases to paste on the wall. Across the street was my grandfather's hardware store. (It was named for him, Jim Morton.) Behind Morton Hardware Company were long sheds where lumber and other supplies were stored. To help his restaurant-owner neighbors, grandfather offered those sheds as a temporary studio for the artist. Apparently the artist was so interesting they moved the canvases to the front store windows so passersby could glimpse his work, too. Although she was not quite ten at the time, Sidney Morton Montgomery remembers every detail of going to the store with her sisters and friends to watch the artist paint the murals. She still enjoys going back to hometown, and the visit must include a meal at the Bright Star and a visit with those still valued paintings of German landscapes.

Sidney Morton Montgomery

Where do my memories begin of the Bright Star? Almost before memory! I remember going to the Bright Star after my very first visit to Dr. Rushing in the Realty Building. I remember meeting my mother, a courthouse employee, at the Bright Star on her payday for lunch. I remember being treated to lunch by General Hanna at the Bright Star with lots of other ladies from Hanna Steel on many occasions. I remember my mother attending both the Retirees Club and Birthday Club with other courthouse employees at the Bright Star. I remember Mother's Day and Father's Day at the Bright Star, as well as Thanksgiving! And loads of "ordinary" days, too. I remember dinner at the Bright Star the day we moved my mother into managed care. I remember my uncle (retired air force) insisting on dining at the Bright Star on every visit home from Oklahoma. The Bright Star is in my memories from the earliest times, and I look forward to many more years of memories of the Bright Star.

Jan Bailey

I wanted to submit a favorite memory of the Bright Star to y'all as you celebrate such an exciting anniversary!

My name is Jeannette Hall and my late husband, Dr. Frank Avery Hall, Sr., and I went to the Bright Star regularly beginning in 1946. Dr. Hall was a dentist in Bessemer until his untimely death in 1963.

One of my fondest memories of the Bright Star is when my husband went deep-sea fishing in the Gulf and we took the fish to the "Star" (Bright Star) and y'all cooked them. We would invite all our friends to eat with us.

I moved to Mobile in 1996, but when I have the pleasure of going back to Bessemer, I always eat at the Bright Star!

Jeannette Hall

My memory of the Bright Star started in 1947, the year my father got killed in a truck wreck. We live in Mobile. Mother, who is now ninety years old, brought us four children back to Bessemer where our families lived. One Saturday in the summer of 1947 Mother put us on the bus and we went to the Grand Theatre in Bessemer. As we were leaving we told Mother we were hungry. We were walking down Nineteenth Street so Mother took all four of us into the Bright Star to eat. Mother ordered us all a hotdog and drink. We all ate. Mother asked the man who waited on our table for the bill. The nice man told her the lunch was paid. He went on to say that we were nice children. That she did not owe anything. That was over fifty-six years ago. I was eleven years old. My name is Janet.

This has been on my mind over the years. I am seventy years old and my brothers and two sisters are still living. They are Basil, Afton, and Loretta. This is what the Bright Star means to my family and me.

I ate lunch in there a week or two ago. I wanted to tell the man and the hostess there my story but I did not. This is the fondest memory of my life.

Janet Humphries

My memories of the Bright Star are totally synonymous with my memories of Bessemer. I lived in Bessemer in the very same house on Sixth Avenue from birth until I left to attend a university out of state. With that, I never lived in Bessemer again, but Bessemer is and will always be my home. Recently, I attended the fortieth reunion of my high school class—the first time I have ever been able to return for a reunion. So many years have gone by; I have lived in many places over these decades—Nashville, Ft. Lauderdale, Charleston, Pensacola, Cincinnati, Indianapolis, and Orlando, and I have now just recently moved back to Alabama (near Mobile)—so the request for stories of the Bright Star seemed to hit a particularly nostalgic note for me. Of all the cities in which I have lived and traveled and their many restaurants, the Bright Star is still the best.

My great-uncle, Jap Bryant, was mayor of Bessemer for a few years and I remember going to the Bright Star with Uncle Jap, my dad (G. C. Hancock, Jr.), and my granddad. Now, I was just a child and their topic of conversation may have been important politics, but I was in a world of my own—looking at the pictures on the wall and being pampered by the waitresses.

My family ate at the Bright Star weekly. It was almost always Friday nights and from my recollection, there were many Bessemer families who did the same. I remember that my dad and mom seemed to know everyone—the Bright Star was a gathering place. We chatted with neighbors or folks who didn't live in Bessemer but just came for the delicious food. I had my first Shirley Temple there—I thought they invented it at the Bright Star just for me! The owner or manager always stopped at our table and chatted—I remember thinking my father was very important for the owner to take such time to make sure our service and food were good. The Bright Star was always the place to be—especially whenever Bama played in Birmingham. You knew you had to get there early or you had no hope of getting in!

After graduating from college and getting married, a visit back to Bessemer always included a meal at the Bright Star. To this day we still plan our travel route through Birmingham with a detour around lunchtime or dinnertime to eat there. I no longer have any relatives in Bessemer, and, sadly, our trip through town includes a visit to the beautiful, peaceful place where my father is buried at Cedar Hill. Last year when we came through, I had two of my grandchildren with me and they loved eating at the Bright Star. That makes at least five generations of our family (that I know of!) who have enjoyed dining at my favorite restaurant.

My best wishes and congratulations to the Bright Star for one hundred years of wonderful memories—and hopes for at least one hundred more!

Brenda Kathryn Hancock Hastings

My name is Amy Holland. My husband, Kevin, and I live in Cullman, Alabama, but we are both originally from Hueytown. We have been married ten years now. It was brought to my attention recently an article you submitted in the Western Star *regarding a book that is to be published about the anniversary of the Bright Star, and for anyone who may have an interesting story about the Bright Star to write and send it to you. Well, I have a romantic story for you. . . .*

The Bright Star holds a very special place in my and my husband's hearts. In mid-November 1993, my husband, Kevin, and I decided to have dinner at the Bright Star to celebrate our two years of dating. Kevin had recently accepted a job in Mobile, Alabama, and would be moving shortly. We had a lot to discuss and celebrate that evening. I opened my anniversary gift from Kevin (the Christmas advent calendar that I had asked for), and as I was looking at each detailed handmade ornament in its own individual pocket I came to the eleventh day and attached to a green ribbon was a gorgeous engagement ring. At that moment he asked me to marry him. Of course I said yes and then I cried as he put the ring on my finger. I remember one of the owners of the Bright Star coming by to congratulate us as did several of the personnel. After a fabulous rehearsal dinner at the Bright Star the evening of March 10, 1995, Kevin and I were married on Saturday, March 11, 1995, at our then hometown church, Pleasant Ridge Baptist in Hueytown.

Now almost eleven years and two kids later (Caroline, age seven, and Grant, age three) we decided to come back to the Bright Star for our tenth anniversary. Of course the food was as fabulous as it has always been. Once again, to my complete surprise, Kevin kneeled down on one knee and proposed to me all over again and asked me to marry him in Las Vegas, Nevada, the following July. I said yes! So, this past July in Las Vegas while attending a pharmacy convention, my husband of ten years and I with our beautiful daughter, Caroline, as my flower girl we renewed our wedding vows in a Las Vegas–style "Elvis" wedding.

I am sure you are receiving many wonderful stories and experiences shared at the Bright Star from different people, but please consider our love story for the book. The Bright Star is a spectacular restaurant and we plan on dining there for years to come.

Kevin and Amy Holland

On her sixteenth birthday, July 10, 1924, my mother, Margaret Elizabeth, was honored with lunch by her parents, Pearl and Frank Turner, at the Bright Star, an exciting restaurant in the City of Bessemer. My grandparents owned a dairy farm outside of town and were very busy and confined. In those days, to dine out in a restaurant was a special treat, and of course a sixteenth birthday for their only daughter called for a special celebration. To leave four brothers at home and dine alone with her parents was a memorable occasion for my mother. Throughout the years, whenever she dined at the Bright Star, she always recalled that special day.

And on April 30, 2005, our precious mother, Margaret Turner Roy, died having blessed her family with ninety-seven years. On May 2, 2005, the day of the private memorial services for her, officiated by Rev. Gordon McKinney at Cedar Hill Cemetery, her family of three daughters, Margaret Ann Griffin (Mack, dec.), Mary Tucker (Tommy, dec.), and Barbara Jordan and Fred, her grandchildren, and great-grandchildren thought it appropriate to celebrate her life with lunch at the Bright Star before the memorial services.

Mr. Jimmy Koikos arranged a private dining area for the family. The lovely atmosphere he created was like that our mother had often planned for her family on special occasions in the dining room of our home.

Many years have passed since that happy sixteenth-birthday celebration, and we believe she would be very pleased with this family occasion celebrating her life. We shared many happy memories of life with our dear mother on that special day.

Margaret Ann Griffin

Dining at the Bright Star was always a treat for my family. And when my three children had their families, they continued to enjoy going to the Bright Star, with their children, while visiting Bessemer. A few years ago, I began a tradition with my grandchildren that I look forward to each Christmas. The Sunday before Christmas, after attending church, we have lunch together at the Bright Star. That first year they were so excited when we gathered together to enjoy this special occasion! As we were busy completing our luncheon orders, the waitress appeared with orders of seafood gumbo for each of us. Smiling, she said, "Compliments of Mr. Eddie Dunlavy for you!" We were delighted with this surprise, and my six grandchildren were certainly impressed with our kind friend's treat. As we have continued to enjoy this tradition of having Sunday Christmas lunch together, some of my grandchildren like to order seafood gumbo, and will often comment, "Grandmother, we like to remember and honor Mr. Dunlavy by ordering this special treat, OK?" They will always treasure his thoughtfulness.

Anonymous

First let us acknowledge that unborn infants can hear their mother's voice and begin bonding with her.

The scene is the Bright Star in June 1948 on a sunny day at lunchtime.

Pam Segars, her pregnant mother, Le Neta, and her Gracemother are being seated for lunch.

Suddenly Pam hears her mother exclaim with pleasure at seeing the fantastic murals on the walls. Her mother, being artistic, found the artwork, the food, and the service all terrific.

That lovely day marks the time Pam Segars (later to add Morris) began to bond big time with her Bright Star and all its people.

Thanks, Bright Star, for many hours of good times and good memories. We all "bonded" with you. We love you today, and will love you more tomorrow.

Le Neta Segars Chapman and all the Segars family

My parents were married on April 22, 1924, at the old Our Lady of Sorrows Church on Avenue F. It was the Tuesday after Easter and the church was filled with Easter lilies and flowers. They had a beautiful wedding and reception. After that they came home to Bessemer to a small house on Sixth Avenue and

Nineteenth Street. The next morning they had a wonderful wedding breakfast at the Bright Star.

The Antonios had a beautiful family of three children: Joseph, born in September 1925; Josephine, born in January 1928; and Betty Jean, born in November 1931.

Being the youngest of these three children, I loved spending special moments with my dad, who was strong, good-looking, and had the best qualities of anyone I knew. He used to take me to the Bright Star to have coffee with him and we would sit at the marble bar on stools and I would struggle with the heavy, big cup to prove how strong I was at four years old. Everyone who came in spoke to my dad—and he was in politics and was an elected official of three terms on the Bessemer City Council as an alderman. He had a wonderful personality and was lovingly called "Johnny." He would introduce me as his "baby daughter Betty."

That was many years ago but a lot of my favorite memories are of being at the Bright Star with my family. They are gone now but I still visit their graves at Cedar Hill and then make my Easter or Christmas luncheon at the Bright Star with my dear husband, Dr. Joe Baldone. I always feel much happier after my visit to Bessemer, after all it was my first home. I will always remember the Bright Star with fond memories of the paintings on the walls. Though they are dim with age, they are still very beautiful to me.

Betty Jean Antonio Baldone

This is a story about me, my husband, and the Bright Star.

We met in a Walgreen's next door to the Bright Star—1943—all the kids went there to hang out. The war was on and we had to do all we wanted to do fast! He was going to go in the air force. We married six weeks later, January 1944.

For our forty-fifth anniversary he took me back where we met. It was a jewelry store then and he bought me earrings. Then he took me to the Bright Star to eat. The jewelry store is now part of the Bright Star.

I am seventy-eight and not a good writer as you can see. This is how we met and the Bright Star was always the special place for us until I lost him in 1990. This helps me go back in time.

Lorene Adkins

I live in Michigan and I visit your restaurant three or four times per year. As soon as I get off of the airplane, my first order of business is to eat at your restaurant. I want you to know that you have some of the best food I have ever tasted, and the service and staff are great! I have been to a lot of places and I have eaten at a lot of restaurants, but no one's food even comes close to yours. I brag about your food to my friends in Michigan. I told them that they haven't tasted great food until they have tasted the Bright Star.

Please continue the great food and good service and you will have me as a customer for life. I'll see you on my next visit.

God bless you.

Mrs. Ennis Byrdsong

After dining out in many restaurants around the city of Birmingham, we settled on the best one and didn't go anywhere else on a Saturday night. This was the Bright Star. At this time, Mr. and Mrs. Bill Koikos were operating the restaurant. They were Nicky and Jimmy's mother and father. Mr. Bill was always on the cash register and as each customer was leaving, Mr. Bill presented this candy dish there on the counter by the register. The dish held small wrapped candies called Nips. As each customer left Mr. Bill would insist we take one. They were small caramels with delicious chocolate inside that would melt in your mouth. Chocolate parfait was our favorite. Today, in 2006, we still enjoy Nips and buy them at CVS drugstores when they are on sale. Too, we still enjoy a small, pocket-size mirror they used to have that had a calendar on it. We still go to the Bright Star when we want to eat out. Why go anywhere else when this is the very best?

Rickie and Byron Wilson

I have been eating at the Bright Star for more than thirty years. Anytime I have guests or customers I always take them there. What I would like to tell you is about an employee that worked there that became a good friend and I miss him. His name is Cliff Isom. He had an accident and his gun went off and killed him [in August 2002]. This is about how I met him.

He had worked as the security there a long time before we met. We would pass each other and say hello and keep on going (he always had a smile for everyone). I was waiting for some people to show up to eat with, and I was standing on the corner looking in the window. It used to be a jewelry shop before it was their lobby. Need to explain something first. I am a businessman in Hueytown but did not look much like one at the time. My hair was halfway down my back and my beard looked like [that of one of the members of] ZZ Top, my favorite group. As I said, I was looking in the window looking at the rings and this guy (drunk) came up to me and put his arm around me and said, "Hey, man, don't you remember me?"

I said, "No." He said, "Yes, we were in jail together." (I have never been in jail at all.) I told him he needed to leave. That is when Cliff came walking up and asked if there was a problem. I said not now. And I told Cliff what the guy had said and he started laughing 'til he almost cried. That is when we first started talking at length with each other.

Another story about Cliff that was so cool is when we were eating there one night and he was sitting at the table with me and a friend of mine came in. I told Cliff, "There is a friend I have not seen in a long time." Cliff asked me what his name was and I told him Ted Quick. Cliff stands up so that Ted could not see me and said, "Hi, Ted, I have not seen you in a long time." Ted did not know what to do because he did not know Cliff or how Cliff knew his name. We had a big laugh out of it.

I now have a new friend at the Bright Star with the same big smile Cliff had. His name is Markus [Marlon Tanksley]. I called him everything but his right name for about a year before I got it right and I am not sure this is how you spell it. If anyone asks me where to eat in the Birmingham area or Bessemer, I always send them or take them to the Bright Star. I feel sorry for Jimmy and Nick. Where do they go to get a better meal? Don't you know they go to some places and wish they were back at the Bright Star.

Steve Sims

I have been coming to the Bright Star for many years. When I'm there I always think of my good friend Barbara Fisher as she loved the Bright Star. I remember special occasions when I've been with "get-togethers" and special reunion events with my Bessemer High School class of 1944.

My mother was a member of the staff in 1944 and threw a graduation party for me and my girlfriends at the Bright Star. That's a memory that I'll never forget. There are so many it's hard to list them all.

There have been anniversary parties for dear friends and thousands of just plain ol' good Bessemer lunches have been enjoyed over the years. And usually Jimmy or his brother, Nick, has been there to greet everyone with a smile and a "How's everything?" Everything is always, always fine.

Also, I have dear memories of Christmas lunches with out-of-town cousins. Everyone always wants to go to the Bright Star. There's never any argument over where to go for a fabulous meal and that "Southern" atmosphere.

When I think of my old hometown of Bessemer, Alabama, where I grew up, the first thing that pops into my head is always . . . the Bright Star.

Thanks to the Star staff, the cooks, and the Koikos family for maintaining such a classic restaurant and a legend in our state and in the entire South.

Norma McDaniel Parsons

I have fond memories of the Bright Star Restaurant. Ralph and I married while he was in the air force. He was discharged in 1946 just before Jean, our daughter, was born. As years passed, we had four sons—Ralph Jr., Clay, Barry, and Peter.

Ralph ate lunch at the Bright Star every day with sales reps and friends who were businessmen. On Sundays, we always went as a family after church.

In 1957 when Ralph Jr. was nine years old, he was diagnosed with a brain tumor. Jimmy and Nicky would tell Ralph they were sending dinner, like turkey and dressing and lots of goodies. They were so thoughtful and we were so appreciative. Things like this you don't forget.

We were privileged to know Mr. and Mrs. Koikos and Helen. They were all so nice. We all have enjoyed the Bright Star and it is still a very special place to eat.

Betty Simmons

I have so many fond memories of the many special occasions with family and friends at the Bright Star over the past fifty years. Our family has spent countless birthdays, anniversaries, and special celebrations at this wonderful gathering place.

I can remember back in the 1950s when my late husband started his law practice just a half block down Third Avenue from the Bright Star having lunch there with him. The food was always great and Mr. and Mrs. Koikos were very hospitable. They were so nice and made you feel like you were eating in their home.

In the years since Jimmy and Nicky took over the restaurant, they continued the excellent service and tradition established by their parents to this day. We watched them mature into fine men and have been very proud of their success.

We always entertained friends and relatives from out of town at the Bright Star. Everyone agreed that the food and atmosphere were excellent.

My late husband ate lunch every weekday at the Bright Star for almost forty-eight years and was honored by Jimmy by reserving "his booth" at the front of the restaurant with his best friends, Jim Gibson and Larry Russell.

I met my friends last week at the Bright Star for lunch. Needless to say, the Bright Star is like home.

Margarete Jackson

My earliest memories as a child of "going out to eat" are of the Bright Star. I really did not know there were other restaurants because "The Star" was where our family went out to eat, special occasions or not. I can remember going to the Bright Star with my dad when I was four or five years old for his midmorning coffee and always knowing that it was a special place. We would sit in our booth and I remember looking up at the murals and thinking I was in a museum. When we went to the counter to pay our bill Mr. Koikos would always give me a piece of candy, which made me feel special.

The Bright Star was a special meeting place for our family over the years, even though my dad had lunch there every workday. My dad continued the tradition of taking my sons to the Bright Star and to this day we all have very favorite memories of eating there. My sons always felt special to have lunch with "Papa."

Two special occasions stand out to me. Breaking with family tradition, in 1995 we went to the Bright Star for Thanksgiving dinner. We all had the six-course turkey and dressing meal, except for my youngest son, Matt. A loyal fan of the Bright Star trout almondine, he refused to break with his tradition even for Thanksgiving.

The other particularly special occasion was the fifteenth birthday of my oldest son, Hall, and our family celebrated another terrific meal. This evening was unique because it happened to be the week Jimmy brought in Jamie Shannon from Commander's Palace to cook with his staff. Our family spent that entire evening enjoying a wonderful meal in our favorite place to eat.

My father passed away in 2002 and the Bright Star remains our family's favorite place to go out to eat, and even though it is not the same, we still have our memories.

The Koikos family have always been perfect hosts and they set the standard for all other restaurants.

Thank you, Jimmy and Nicky. We wish you continued success.

Tom Jackson

We've had many great occasions at the Bright Star, but this is my favorite.

We belong to a local camping club called Rolling Wheels. I had called to make reservations for our group to have lunch and a meeting. Upon arriving, I checked with the waitress about seating our group. She looked at us, then said, "Oh my goodness, we set up your group as being handicapped!" They thought Rolling Wheels meant wheelchairs. We all had a good laugh.

Janice Hulgan

For more than twenty years the Bright Star Restaurant has been our family's special place. On the Monday before Christmas each year, my three brothers, their wives, my wife, and I have lunch at the Bright Star.

About eleven years ago my eldest brother passed away in July, but we continued the tradition. The next year in September, a sister-in-law passed away, but we continued the tradition. Now I have a terminal illness called myelodysplastic syndromes, a form of cancer of the bone marrow. I would certainly like to be able to make next Christmas lunch with the remainder of my family, but of course that is in God's hands.

John Lee Armstrong

Eating at the Bright Star once a week is a tradition with my mom and me. Every week we share trout almondine and shredded cabbage with dressing on the side. Mom always gets creamed corn and fried okra. I usually get a veggie plate: field peas, greens, corn, and fried okra. We take out lemon icebox pie. We love the Bright Star because all the employees are so nice and friendly and the food is outstanding. Congratulations on the Bright Star's one-hundredth anniversary in 2007. We hope you continue to stay in business so that future generations can enjoy the special treat of lunch in Bessemer at the Bright Star.

Cathy Hansberry

Lemon Icebox Pie

Carlos Starks, who makes the Bright Star's pies, always has to produce a few extra lemon icebox pies—several of this favorite are ordered to go every day.

4 14-ounce cans sweetened condensed milk, chilled
4 egg yolks, slightly beaten
1 cup freshly squeezed lemon juice, chilled
2 9-inch graham cracker crumb piecrusts, homemade or store-bought
1 can whipped cream for topping

Mix sweetened condensed milk and egg yolks together in a bowl. Add lemon juice to mixture in a steady stream while whisking until well blended. Mixture will thicken. Pour into piecrusts. Refrigerate 1 hour or more. Top with whipped cream before serving.

Makes 2 9-inch pies

Being born and raised in Bessemer, Alabama, there was only one nice restaurant to enjoy. That, of course, was the Bright Star. Yes, we had the Town Clock Cafeteria, McClellan's sandwich counter, the Post House, etc., but nothing could ever compare to visiting the Bright Star.

My first memories of this Bessemer treasure were when I was a little girl. Mr. Koikos would always give me a cigar box to use at school to hold my pencils and crayons. After eating there, he would always treat me to an after-dinner mint. I know this isn't much today, but to a little girl it was something special. He was such a lovely, gentle man.

My mother always spent her morning and afternoon coffee breaks at "The Shining Star." This was my mother's affectionate name for the Bright Star. It was a special treat for me to go with her. She would have her coffee and I would have a small Coke. Occasionally, she would let me get a dish of vanilla ice cream. Now this was a special treat!

This was the meeting place for the folks that worked in town. I can remember such folks as Mayor Lanier, Zeke Jordan, Jimmy and Katherine Gibson, Roger and Frances Thames, Ashley Nolan, Mr. and Mrs. Seymour, Mr. and Mrs. Sokol, and the list could go on and on forever. Even a celebrity or two could be spotted inside. Over the years I have seen Ray Perkins, Bart Starr, and other celebrities enjoying the atmosphere. Folks at the Bright Star expect anyone who is there to dine on a scrumptious meal, even the well recognized!

Remember now, the Bright Star was and still is the only fine restaurant in town. My mother was always elated when Reverend Jordan ended our Presbyterian church service around 11:45. That way, the Presbyterians were able to beat the Methodists and Baptists for Sunday lunch. Mr. Jordan always preached the "three b's." Be quick, be brief, be gone! Sunday lunch was always the most favorite meal there in the Jenkins household.

Mother's Day and Easter Sundays were always the favorite days for my family to dine with the Koikos family. You had to get there early or you were simply out of luck! My most poignant memory was the first Mother's Day after my mother passed away. I took my father there to enjoy a delicious meal. Daddy was down and understandably so. I noticed behind us to our left an old classmate of mine. I did not say anything but simply wrote on my Daddy's placemat (this upside down) "Ellen's X" followed by an arrow pointing in that direction. Poor Daddy. "Ellen's X what?" he exclaimed loudly. No, he was not quiet about it. Bless my classmate's heart. Frank came to the table and expressed his sympathy to my father about the loss our family had experienced. Daddy shed a tear, as did I, but it was and still is a most enjoyable memory. Whenever I think about this incident, I can't help but get a chuckle, especially remembering the look on Daddy's face when he realized what "Ellen's X" meant.

The Bright Star has long been a staple in the lives of Bessemer folk! Teachers go there to enjoy a nice, delicious lunch on teacher workdays. Red Hat gals love to get together to relax and enjoy the nice service and chat about the goings-on in our lives. The Bright Star is a great place to celebrate birthdays and anniversaries, to plan high school reunions, to celebrate any special occasion or no special occasion at all. Just enjoy the array of delicious Greek food, ambience, and make new memories.

Thank you, Jimmy and Nicky, for the many happy, glorious memories I will hold dear in my heart for many years to come!

Paula Jenkins McPoland

We have come to the Bright Star for so many years and have many stories to tell.

When I first met Eddie Allison, my husband, he was involved in racing with his brothers. This was in 1967. They would come back into town late on Sunday night after a race. Bobby would call the Bright Star and Jimmy and Nicky would always wait for them to get there and serve them, no matter how late. Probably shouldn't tell this part, but . . . this was back in the time of no alcohol sales on Sunday. Bobby always liked to have one beer when he got in. They would serve it to him in a hot teapot and coffee cup!!

After Eddie and I had our son in 1981, we started taking him to the Bright Star when he was three weeks old. We would go on a weeknight when it wasn't so crowded. Dear, sweet Anne Mull would hold him and play with him while we ate. We forgot his pacifier one night, and Eddie had to go back home and get it. We wouldn't have made it through that night without Anne! She watched Jacob grow up all the way through college. We didn't think we could be served by anyone but her.

When Jacob's third birthday was coming up, my father told him he would take him anywhere he wanted to go for this birthday. Well, it was the "White Star" for "frimp." That's exactly where we went. He is twenty-four now, and it's still his favorite place to go.

My late father-in-law, the great "Pop" Allison, loved the Bright Star also. We would go as a large family for Easter, Mother's Day, etc. Everyone ordered from the lunch menu except Dad—he always got the filet! No sissy lunches for him!

The only person we know who is still alive and older than the Bright Star is the "matriarch" of the Allison family, Mom (Kittie) Allison. She will turn one hundred on October 12, 2006. She, like the rest of us, considers the Bright Star her favorite place. That says a lot, being that she was one of the best cooks ever.

The Bright Star is just such a wonderful place to go. When you walk in the door, everyone makes you feel like you are walking into your own home for a fine dinner.

We look forward to many more years of very good dining with you all.

Congratulations!

Penny Allison

Jimmy, Nicky, and Helen have done a wonderful job of running the Bright Star for so many years. Their parents would be so proud of them. It is one of the finest restaurants anywhere. I used to tell Jimmy every time I ate there, "I hope I eat at the Bright Star the night before I die!"

Linda Horton Mendel

I have been a customer of the Bright Star Restaurant for over twenty-five years. What I remember most is how special I feel when the owners are the ones that seat you and check on you to make sure everything is perfect. You don't see that much anymore. The Bright Star is truly Bessemer's treasure and one of my favorite places to eat. The Bright Star gets a "Gold Star" in my book.

Lana Smitherman

After thirty or more years of going to the Bright Star, it is hard to know where to begin.

When John was working as a buyer at U.S. Steel, he ate lunch there almost daily. He had his own booth known as "Mr. John's" booth, and also during that time we celebrated all special occasions—birthdays, anniversaries—at the Bright Star.

We have fond memories of Papa and Mama Koikos, and the wonderful bread she baked for us, and once a Greek dish we enjoyed.

We remember Nita Ray and Sherry (now Parsons) who gave us wonderful service and made us feel special.

Our fifty-fifth wedding anniversary was a big party with all of our large family, and it was really special.

During John's working years we took all visitors to the Bright Star, and they were duly impressed. Salesmen from Chicago and Texas. The latter was the cause of the "Texas Special" now on the menu, because he asked for steak and fish, and Jimmy obliged.

We have taken personal friends from Nevada, Seattle, Washington, D.C., Arkansas, Missouri, Florida, and Tennessee and were never disappointed.

Now that John has retired we are unable to go as often as we did through the years, but it is like a homecoming when we do. We are made to feel so welcome and special.

The word "special" seems to be overused here, but that is what the Bright Star, Jimmy, and Nicky are—part of our extended family and an important part of our lives, and "special."

John and Catherine Fievet

During the night I thought of someone who needs to be remembered in the book. She was part of my pleasant memories of the Bright Star—sweet Mary Warren. She always greeted me with a kiss on the cheek and said, "Hello, pretty lady!"

Everyone grieved for Mary when she was taken so suddenly and tragically.

Catherine Fievet

We called ourselves the "Kiss My Grits Gang" (six to eight people). We always requested Anne "Flo" Mull. We tried to get the best of her, but she always got the upper hand. We sure do miss her.

Another time we brought in a married couple from England to the restaurant. The husband was a bobby, or policeman, in London. The security guard there at the time (the late Cliff Isom) wanted his picture taken with the man from England. We gave him a copy of the picture, which he seemed delighted to have. This security guard was always so kind and always remembered us on arrival.

Lane Gibbs and Fred Blevins

I just wanted to write a quick thank you for your kindness and hospitality at the Bright Star Restaurant recently. My friends and I were delighted by the truly unique meal, and will not soon forget it. Presiding over the Senate to hear Senator Heflin's description of your many fine dishes some twelve years ago left a lasting impression on me, and I am pleased to have finally sampled your restaurant personally. Senator Heflin was right—the food was some of the best I have ever had. Thank you again for the terrific experience. I hope to make it back soon and look forward to seeing you then.

Senator Russ Feingold

I wish that I could say that I witnessed this incident; but I have heard several who did tell and retell this account many times. I know all who were present so I must submit this anonymously.

Three couples drove fifty miles in one car to Bessemer for a Sunday evening dinner at the Bright Star. As usual they had to wait for a table in the back left dining room. I guess this one guy got hungry. Finally being shown to their table, as he passed the kitchen window where orders were waiting to be picked up and served, he snatched a fried shrimp from someone else's plate. Shortly afterward, he realized this had been witnessed by Jimmy or Nicky, who promptly escorted him out the front door where he was told not to come back to the Bright Star.

I was told that his friends and his wife were greatly amused and stayed for a wonderful dinner while he sat in the car on the street.

Anonymous

I have so many fond memories of eating and visiting with friends at the Bright Star that it is hard to compile them in this letter. My first visit to Bright Star was approximately thirty-eight years ago and my husband and I felt the week was not complete without a meal at "The Star."

As years passed we ate with many friends and family members. We would often say, "Do you want the best food in the South or do you want ambience?" Usually the answer was "good food." This leads me to the one special memory I want to share.

We were hosting a large group of friends for a special event and Jim (my husband, who died five years ago) ordered snapper throats. He whispered to me that they were not as good as usual. No one else heard this and we continued our meal. However, within a minute or two, Nick reached over Jim's shoulder and said, "Mr. Phillips, those snapper throats don't look exactly right. They look a little too dark to be good and so I had them cook you another order." We were speechless . . . we had not complained . . . we had not said a word to Nick . . . we did not expect another meal . . . Nick just observed this on his own and replaced the meal. We were taken by surprise!

At the Bright Star we have observed anniversary and birthday parties, as well as hosting dinner parties; we have eaten with Sunday school classes, Dutch supper clubs, family members, and friends; and we have had our own "supper" together, always with the assurance of a good meal. One of our favorite things was to bring out-of-town family members to eat at "The Star," knowing that we would not be disappointed.

Since Jim's death, I have not been as often as I would like; however, anytime I can get there, especially at lunchtime, I take advantage of the opportunity. Jimmy and Nick are always warm, friendly, and kind. The service is always prompt and the food simply delicious. The Bright Star holds a special place in my life and I look forward to being part of their "food family" for many years.

Mrs. Margaret Phillips

My husband, Ernest Armstrong, worked in the Raymond Ore Mines in 1932. He broke his back and was paralyzed from his hip down. He was in Bessemer General Hospital six months and passed away May 25, 1933.

I would walk up to the Bright Star the days I sat with him. You made English pea soup that was the best tasting I ever ate. I was pregnant with my fourth son. It was in the depression days and not much money in. Can't remember the price but know it wasn't very much. Only knew it was good. I am looking to celebrate my one-hundredth birthday on October 28, 2006, at the Oaks in Parkwood.

Willie Mae Phillips

It is with great pleasure to send our congratulations on one hundred years of service. There is something remarkable and unique about a family-owned business. We treasure the friendship and memories we have shared with the Bright Star family over the years. The Bright Star family and the Joy Young family always enjoyed dining out in each other's restaurant. Our children have literally grown up at the Bright Star. They started going to the Bright Star as infants. As they got older, it was always their first choice when asked where they wanted to go out to eat. They are now twenty-three and twenty-one years old. It continues to be their favorite restaurant. The Joy Young family has had many family celebrations at the Bright Star. What wonderful times we have had! Thanks to the entire staff of the Bright Star for being part of our special family memories. We feel very fortunate to be part of this history.

Henry and Louise Joe
Suelin and Lindsay
Joy Young Restaurant

I can't specify any particular visit to Bright Star as a special occasion, since every visit was a "special occasion." The food was always excellent, the service (especially when we had Anne [Mull] as our waitress, who was also always fun) was the best, and everything became an enjoyable experience.

Whenever we had out-of-town visitors, dinner at Bright Star was a must; it was a chance to show friends that we had first-class restaurants in Alabama.

Congratulations on one hundred years and many more.

Cecelia and Phil Marcoux

My grandmother Pauline Skinner had her first visit on her seventieth birthday for lunch. Jimmy came over to say hello. As we were finishing our meal a birthday dessert came to our table for her.

The smile on her face and the light in her eyes when she realized that "nice man" knew it was her birthday and treated her to lunch on the house was priceless.

That's one she never forgot and I never will. Of all my stories of the years at the Bright Star, this one is my favorite.

Paula Armstrong Smith

I am writing this letter in memory of Ila Patton, affectionately known as "Granny." If Granny were living she would be writing this letter. For seventeen years, we drove from Clanton to Hueytown to bring Granny to the Bright Star for lunch almost every week. Granny loved the Bright Star and we share her enthusiasm for it. The food was always superior to all the other restaurants and in addition to excellent food, the personnel was always kind and friendly. In fact, Granny always managed to get the attention of Jim or the chef to tell them she enjoyed her lunch. We were allowed to sit at the same table week after week. Jim once told us he thought we owned that table. That really pleased Granny. On a number of occasions, we celebrated Granny's birthday at the Bright Star. The service was always outstanding and the staff always seemed to enjoy the party with friends and family. Had Granny been well on her ninetieth birthday, I'm sure she would have wanted to celebrate it at the Bright Star.

We still return to the Bright Star every chance we get to enjoy the food, the kindness of the staff, and our fond memories of "Granny" and the Bright Star.

I would like to congratulate the Bright Star Restaurant for its years of outstanding food and service.

Faye M. Brown

My mother and father took me as a small child to the Bright Star in the early 1940s. My favorite things to eat then were the tenderloin of trout (that was what it was called back then—not trout almondine) and the steak served on a sizzling platter. You could hear the waitress approaching your table with the steak sizzling and popping on the meal platter. Back then there was always olive oil and vinegar served in cruets on each table—no fancy salad dressings.

When I married I took my two sons there to eat and they dearly loved it and still do. About that time Mrs. Koikos made homemade bread for the whole restaurant. It was delicious! One of my sons now lives in South Carolina and the other lives in Virginia. They do not get red snapper, the Gulf shrimp, and oysters in their states. We in Alabama do not realize how fortunate we are to have the Gulf seafood. Now when they are in Bessemer, my grandchildren eat at the Bright Star and love it.

So this is the fourth generation of my family to enjoy the many good dishes.

Jo Ann Barr

Mary Helen Warren had five brothers: the Parks boys—Dalton, Roger, Jerry, John, and Ray. She also had one sister, Wanda Philpott. She was a waitress at the Bright Star until her death in a house fire just a few years ago. She was a very sweet and caring person. We all have fond memories of Mary Helen talking about how she enjoyed working at the Bright Star.

Roger and Diane Parks

The Bright Star has been on my mind along with Bessemer, my dear friends, and my sister being gone. It occurred to me that the Bright Star has been there through three generations of the happy and the sad times of my family. Mother and Daddy lunched on "meat and three" so many times. My children remember always going to the Bright Star during our summer visits from California many times and [flying] back to California with three children and two quarts of gumbo! Once, Mother and I left the hospital while Daddy was so ill. We were bone tired and had dinner at the Bright Star. When the time came to pay, Mr. Bill said it was "on the house" and served us brandy. And, of course, our favorite story is about the Sunday we were all there for lunch and the waitress said, "Your usual, Mrs. Guyton?" She brought Mother her bourbon in a coffee cup!

There are so many stories. Mother and I used to go to early morning mass and would walk over to the Bright Star for breakfast and Miss Tasia would bring fresh bread to us. So warm and delicious! Our reward for walking to and from St. Aloysius.

The memories are so wonderful and always bring a smile to my face.

We are counting on the Bright Star to be there when I bring my grandchildren and Margaret and Johnny's two great-grandchildren. They were all together this past Christmas. I'm so glad.

Mary Sue Guyton Griffin

Do you want to know how to keep from getting homesick for your favorite restaurant? Do what I did. I bought a set of the dinner plates my favorite restaurant, the Bright Star, uses. They are the white round plates and white oval platters, both of which have the beautiful green Bright Star logo on them and have served so many delicious meat and fish entrees through the years. Now on those rare occasions when I cook at home, I serve the meal on those gleaming white plates and immediately the appearance of what I cooked takes on a whole new look!

While all of that helps with appearance, nothing can imitate the wonderful atmosphere at 304 Nineteenth Street North in Bessemer. The quality of food prepared by the efficient staff in the kitchen and the graciousness of the fun servers in the dining rooms make eating with Jimmy and Nicky Koikos a dining experience! Is it any wonder this fine restaurant has been around for one hundred years?

Joy E. Murray

Our daughter and her husband (Leigh and Drew Bardenwerper) were married at the Bright Star Restaurant on August 19, 2005. One of their first dates was there, and they fell in love with the elegance of the restaurant. They both wanted a memorable, cozy, sit-down dinner wedding and immediately thought of the Bright Star. The atmosphere, food, and service were absolutely perfect. Many guests told us of their fond memories of eating at the restaurant in the past. Others told us that they had heard of the historic restaurant and were anxious to attend the wedding.

Brenda Salser made planning the wedding stress free. She and her professional staff accommodated us in every way.

Leigh and Drew have dined at the Bright Star several times since they married and plan to celebrate their first and many more anniversaries at your wonderful restaurant.

Sherry and Denney Owen

In 1954, Sandy Thompson, David Farr, Royce Braden, "John Boy" Rockett, and I were sharing 2 Cokes at the Bright Star when David dared me to stand up and start singing. I saw a table of Italian Americans and started singing "That's Amore." Immediately Mr. Koikos started heading my way and everyone ran except me. Mr. Koikos didn't like any nonsense in his restaurant, but the Italian family started applauding. To my surprise, Mr. Koikos said, "You know any Greek song?" I replied, "No, but I can learn." He told me to come back when I learned a Greek song and tell my friends to bring enough money for four Cokes because mine would be "on the house."

I didn't go back for two years!

Gloria Ann Campbell Parks

My memory of the Bright Star is of camping Thanksgiving week at Tannehill State Park and having Thanksgiving dinner with friends and family at the Bright Star. This mirror was given to me by our good neighbor Nick Costas. He and Cleo are such good neighbors and friends.

Dot LeCroy

On Thanksgiving Day 1996 our family decided to spend our time together for lunch at the Bright Star. We both had dined there for many years. Our neighbor of an area near Bessemer was a recent widow and had fond memories of the restaurant also. She enjoyed company and we were delighted when she accepted the invitation to go with us. She had said to have a meal there was the Brightest Star in her week. We chose our favorites: the Texas Special, snapper throats, Greek-style snapper, famous slaw, pineapple-cheese pie, chocolate silk pie, and of course cornbread was a treat too.

We always went with great anticipation and excitement to see familiar faces that served so caringly, and Nick was always gracious when he saw us.

We wish there were more people in the world like these have been in our lives—to be interested in the quality of food and service. Our best wishes for another century.

Cile and Stuart Leach

My favorite memory is of Miss Anne [Mull] and all the hugs she gave our son Nathan. If we could not get in her section, he went to her to get a hug.

Betty Bucks

My brother-in-law, Earl Cornelius Cull, helped restore the paintings around the top of the main dining room. I am not sure of the year. I believe he worked for a gentleman by the name of Jack Costello, a painting contractor, who lived in the Bessemer area at the time. We love to eat at the Bright Star and always admire the paintings. Earl Cull is now deceased—he went by the name of Neal Cull.

Mr. Costello died about thirteen years ago, but his wife still lives in the Bessemer house where she and Mr. Costello raised seven daughters during his long painting career. Jack and their family were longtime friends of Jimmy and Nick Koikos. Jack had handled all their personal and business painting needs over a period of years. They trusted Jack to handle the mural restoration.

Earl always attributed everything he knew about painting to Jack. Earl was an excellent painter, a very hard worker, and I'm sure when Jack took on the restoration, he felt Earl was very capable and would contribute a great deal to this project. Earl spoke to my husband, Ted, often about the murals. He was very proud of the job they had done. My husband recalls Earl said the plaster was crumbling behind the murals and he used hypodermic needs to inject glue behind the paintings to stabilize them. Earl died in 1996.

Mary Frances and Ted Cull

Every Thursday my mother, Margaret McClinton, my aunt Lucile Flynn, and two other lifelong friends since childhood (Maude Cowen and Florence Russell) would drive from Hueytown to the Bright Star. They were all retired teachers and were all "seniors."

They would arrive before you opened for lunch so they could find a close parking place. Mrs. Koikos would always meet them at the front door . . . sometimes letting them in early. She always greeted them with "I already have your decaf coffee ready." Her graciousness was a perfect beginning to a delicious lunch that they looked forward to for many, many years. They always ordered trout almondine and carrot and raisin salad. And on one of their birthdays, they allowed themselves a delicious piece of pie!

Although all four are no longer with us, we remember how much they looked forward to their "outing" and the memories are precious.

You are a wonderful part of the Birmingham area and of our families' lives. May God bless you!

Martha (McClinton) and Rob Langford

The Bright Star has been my favorite for seventy-nine years. I am eighty-four years old now and I can remember when I was five years old, living in Bessemer on Grandeville Avenue. At the time, my father would come by the Bright Star and buy lunch for himself, my mother, and me. He would have to hurry to get to the Bright Star, to our home, eat lunch, and get back downtown to work on time. We always looked forward to this treat. I grew up loving the Bright Star.

I have fond memories of special occasions, birthdays, anniversaries, etc., during my teenage years at the Bright Star.

When I married, my husband had never eaten at the Bright Star (he was from north Alabama). I quickly acquainted with this fine restaurant. When he learned how much it meant to me, we ate there often. We always celebrated our anniversary there.

After my husband died in 1993, I don't get to eat there as often, but I go every chance I get. I ate there today. About thirty minutes after I got home, a friend called and said, "Would you like to go to the Bright Star for lunch tomorrow?" I replied, "You bet!" So I ate there today and I will eat there tomorrow. It is great food and service every time I go.

Mrs. Jessie C. Terry

Some of the best memories we have of the Bright Star center around my parents, Elizabeth and Jimmy Walsh. Elizabeth and Jimmy were Bright Star regulars for well over thirty years. In recent years, they always wanted to be served by Neda Arthur because of her service, her friendly smile, and the pampering she always gave to them. During this time period, my husband and I, along with our two young sons, spent many of our Sundays waiting while others were seated just so we could be served by Neda. Many times, on special days like Easter or Mother's Day, we found ourselves sitting outside, sometimes for several hours, just to get inside the Bright Star and sit in Neda's section. My parents have both passed away and our sons are now grown and are out on their own, but my husband and I still come to the Bright Star every Sunday. We still like the service we receive from Neda but we also like to sit in other sections as well. Everyone who serves at the Bright Star is always friendly, courteous, and helpful. The food is always great but what keeps us coming back are the people who work at the Bright Star. From Mr. Jimmy right on down the line, there is no better restaurant in the South than the Bright Star.

Linda Walsh Ponder
Reese, Hunter, and Scott

On our yearly visit [from Cincinnati, Ohio] to Mr. and Mrs. Murray Armstrong of Trussville, Alabama, we look forward to dining at your wonderful restaurant. We appreciate your superior food, outstanding service, and overall Southern hospitality. It is unusual to find such a gem in a small town.

We were there on Friday, May 12, 2006, and learned that a major milestone is ahead of you in 2007. It is quite an accomplishment to celebrate your one-hundredth anniversary. What a wonderful history your place has!

May these first one hundred years of success serve as the inspiration for the next one hundred years.

Our best wishes and congratulations to all of you on this exceptional event. We look forward to seeing you again soon!

Dr. and Mrs. Mitchell Ede

Candied Yams

Just as in the 1950s Bright Star kitchen, whole yams are peeled and sliced for this recipe, which is the one most requested by customers. The slight tang of fresh lemon juice complements the traditional sweet ingredients of candied yams.

Approximately 5 pounds of sweet potatoes, peeled
1 1/2 cups granulated sugar
1/3 cup lemon juice
1/4 cup vanilla extract
1 tablespoon cinnamon
1/2 tablespoon nutmeg
2 sticks butter (cut into slices)
1 cup water

Preheat oven to 350°. Parboil sweet potatoes for 30 minutes and drain. When cooled, slice into 1/2-inch pieces, and place in a 9 x 13 pan. Sprinkle the remaining ingredients over sweet potatoes. Cover with foil. Bake at 350° for 45 minutes.

Serves 8–10.

Growing up in the 1960s and early 1970s and living approximately two miles from downtown Bessemer, my family and I were fortunate to frequent the Bright Star Restaurant just about every weekend. Eating supper there was, I guess you could say, our Saturday night ritual. Although there was a wide variety of items on the menu to choose from, my mother and I usually had the fried shrimp and my father loved the hamburger steak smothered in onions and gravy. It was such a treat to eat there and even as a child I remembered getting the sense that it was really an upscale restaurant but yet the owners and employees stopped at our table frequently to talk with us and treated us like part of the family.

Sadly, when I became a teenager, I thought I was too old to go out to eat with my parents and I cheated myself out of many more wonderful dining experiences. If I had known then what I know now, I would have never passed up an opportunity to eat at the Bright Star! Many years have passed and the restaurant is larger in size than it was over thirty years ago, but the atmosphere, quality of food, and the attention given to serving the customers remain unchanged to this day.

Lisa Warren Poole
In honor of Lois Warren and the late Buford Warren of Bessemer

When I saw your notice in the restaurant about the book you are putting together, I felt compelled to write about how the Bright Star has been a tradition in our family. It was started by my grandparents, Sam and Marie Ciulla, fifteen to twenty years ago. They loved coming to the restaurant for lunch. Their dining choice was almost always the same: snapper throats (broiled, not fried), candied yams, and whatever other vegetable struck their fancy that day. We all knew that the Bright Star was their favorite place to eat, so we enjoyed many family get-togethers there over the years: their anniversary, Father's Day, Mother's Day, birthdays. And you were all so kind to accommodate us, which was a small feat considering that we number close to fifty when we all get together.

My grandmother died three years ago this September. Although the rest of us continue to frequent your fabulous restaurant, my grandfather never felt the same about going there after her death. You see, he has always considered the Bright Star "their place," and it just didn't seem right for him to go without her. Thank you, Jimmy and Nick, for some wonderful memories that all of us will cherish forever.

Lisa Hoyle

The Bright Star has been an important part of our family dining tradition since 1925. My grandfather and grandmother, Newborn and Alice Riley, would bring me to the restaurant for a late lunch every other Saturday. Newborn was a rural letter carrier and had to take care of his horse, which pulled the mail wagon, before setting out for food in his brand-new Model T Ford.

As time passed, I worked at Woodward Iron Company and would stop by home and bring my son Greek salads as a treat. Now my grandson, who is a contractor in Birmingham, brings my great-grandchildren to the Bright Star for some of the same great food that their great-great-great-grandparents enjoyed.

We had an early Father's Day lunch today, and I heard about the letters you were soliciting about memories of your restaurant and couldn't resist writing.

Congratulations and all the best for another one hundred years!

Stancel M. Riley

In February 2006, the Burgoff's, my favorite restaurant in Chicago, closed its doors for the final time. I have mourned the passing of many of my favorite eateries over the years, and those sad experiences truly make me appreciate the longevity of the Bright Star. Since I grew up in Birmingham's West End and had several relatives in Bessemer, it was natural that our family would dine at the Bright Star with great frequency. My wife grew up in Tuscaloosa and had relatives in Birmingham, so she also starting eating at the Bright Star as a small child.

We lived in Jacksonville, Florida, for eighteen years, and I worked at the Seaboard Coast Line Railroad's headquarters. In December 1987, I made an inspection trip on a freight train that went through Bessemer at night when the streets were pretty deserted. There were lots of cars around the Bright Star, however, and I could see the big neon star over the restaurant's old entrance. I was hungry anyway, and that made me wish that I could swing down off the locomotive and walk up the street for one of those great Greek-style snappers!

My most poignant memory of the Bright Star relates to my father's final years when he was afflicted with Alzheimer's disease. Dad had been co-captain of his college football team, and he had been a businessman for fifty-seven years, so it was hard on all of us to see him in that condition. It was difficult to take him out to eat as his condition progressed, but I always felt comfortable about taking him to the Bright Star. He loved going back to the Bright Star, and everyone always treated him with kindness and dignity.

Congratulations to everyone at the Bright Star on the restaurant's one-hundredth birthday. I hope this great Bessemer institution will be around many more years for our children and grandchildren.

Lyle Key

I had finished my surgery residency at the end of June 1975 and immediately began my private practice at what was then East End Memorial Hospital. It was a "solo" practice with little free time to enjoy things other than family, until Anastasia Koikos came into my life. What a great friend she became.

She had been evaluated for an intestinal problem that had been diagnosed as needing surgical intervention. She was referred to me by her daughter and son-in-law, Helen and John Cocoris. The procedure was a success, but the follow-up visits created lasting memories I shall carry the rest of my life.

On each visit, she would arrive with the "world famous" pineapple-cheese pie from the Bright Star Restaurant. What a treat, and what a visit we would have, talking about families and everything else in the world, at least long enough for me to fall way behind in seeing other patients in the office. But the special surprise came one day when she arrived with a handmade knitted shawl for my little two-year-old daughter, Heather. It was yellow and precious on my beautiful little girl. But then, one month later, she came back for a social visit, and had knitted another one in brown.

My daughter wore them a great deal, as we were so proud of them. She now has her own little girl, Addison, who loves wearing them and is just as precious. Mrs. Koikos's friendship and gifts have been passed through two generations, and will certainly continue to affect many more.

Dr. William C. "Bucky" Wood

I would like to write about the special friendship between Mrs. Tasia Koikos and my mother, Christine Catechis Louzis.

In 1928, my mother, Christine, age twelve, left the island of Corfu, Greece, with her parents. She met another twelve-year-old girl, Anastasia (Tasia Microyiannakis), who was traveling with her uncle, George Koutroulakis, and his bride, Eugenia, from Laconia, Greece. On the ship they became fast friends when they realized they were heading to the same place—Birmingham, Alabama.

Christine and Tasia had much in common. Christine was a bridesmaid in Tasia and Bill's wedding. They each married in 1936 and had three children. As the oldest, I was taught to call Mrs. Koikos, "Thea," or Aunt Tasia, and Mr. Koikos, Uncle Bill, even though we were not related. I lived on Norwood Circle in Birmingham, and Helen, "Thea" Tasia's oldest child, in Bessemer. We are lifelong friends like our mothers and so are our daughters, Mary Chris and Stacey.

She and her brothers, Jim and Nick, would come visit and I would go to Bessemer by streetcar with my mother, my sister, Mary, and my brother, Manuel, and spend the entire day playing house, kickball, and running outside.

When I married John Dikis, we moved to Jasper, Alabama, for a short time. Helen and Jimmy drove down in his new Chevrolet convertible to see me. Jimmy would park his car in the carport in case it rained.

Tasia and Bill Koikos and Christine and George Louzis took trips to Tarpon Springs for the Feast Day of Epiphany on January 6 and had many amusing adventures. My mother would also meet "Thea" Tasia at Joy Young's, a restaurant in Birmingham, for lunch and a whiskey sour. They had such fun and always were like young girls when they were together. They enjoyed being members of "Knit- Chat-Chew" [social club] along with other friends of their era and had lunch at each other's houses.

Though our mothers have passed away, Christine in 1984 and "Thea" Tasia in 1989, Helen and I share many happy memories of our mothers.

Georgia Louzis Dikis

The Bright Star is, of course, a wonderful restaurant that provides excellent food and service. However, it is much more to me. It is and has always been a place of comfort that has provided more than nourishment for the body. Its stability and familiar surroundings have provided me with pleasure and comfort through the best and worst times of my life.

When I enter the Bright Star, I feel good. I am always greeted in a manner that makes me feel welcome and, in some way, a part of the Bright Star. I am entering a place that has been a part of my life for most of my life, a part that has been consistent and unchanging.

And at times it has been a place of refuge. When my wife, Toolie, was very ill, we could always go to the Bright Star and escape for a while. No matter what else was happening, we could lose ourselves for a while in the warm, comfortable surroundings. We would enjoy the wonderful food and the warmth of the Koikos family.

An atmosphere such as this does not just happen—it comes from the family. It is this attitude that is the basis for the Bright Star. It is this attitude that produces the wonderful food and service. It is this caring attitude that I believe that you can taste in the food, the attention to detail, and the desire to please (every person and every order is important).

As you can surmise, I love the Bright Star. I love the food, and I love the people. Congratulations on one hundred years, and thank you for many wonderful memories.

Tommy Buttram

Around the turn of the twentieth century, my grandfather, George L. (Boss) Bell, ran a livestock business on First Avenue and Nineteenth Street in Bessemer. He had a livestock lot on the corner of Twentieth Street and First Avenue. My mother, Margaret (Sue) Bell Kachelhofer, told me that many times as a child she would go to the Bright Star and would sit in her daddy's lap for lunch at the restaurant. She said that a Saturday's entertainment would be walking from their home on Fairfax Avenue to have lunch at the Bright Star and then go to a movie at the Grand Theatre. We moved away from Bessemer in the late 1950s, but still enjoy the Bright Star on visits to Bessemer. My father is ninety years old and when he visits here, the only place for a family gathering is the Bright Star.

Robert Kachelhofer, Jr.

My father did electrical work for the Bright Star. I had my first meal at the Star when I was around five years old; this would have been sixty-five years ago. I went along with him while he was repairing a fan in the kitchen, and the cook gave me a drumstick and fries.

I still eat at the Star and enjoy the best food around.

Rudy Sheehan

My husband first took me to the Bright Star almost thirteen years ago for our anniversary. We go every year for that specific date and many other dates in between. The food is always superb. The service is always above and beyond the call. We drive almost an hour to eat there and would drive further if we had to. So glad you are a great restaurant; there aren't very many to equal yours.

Carla Ann Sexton

The Bright Star was a Christmas Eve tradition when I was growing up in Bessemer with my family, starting about forty years ago. My parents, my brother, and I had dinner at the Bright Star every Christmas Eve for most of my childhood. I can still remember the taste of the veal with cream sauce that was my favorite dish. After dinner was a walk down Nineteenth Street to do some last-minute window-shopping and to just enjoy the sights and sounds of Christmas with family. It is a memory I will never forget, even though I no longer live in Alabama.

Susan Dournaux

My husband, Jim Ed, and I love the Bright Star. In fact, five generations of our family have enjoyed the hospitality, the social life, and the food at the Bright Star.

Mr. and Mrs. Koikos were the most gracious and sincere couple I have ever known. In the 1950s and 1960s, when we arrived at the Bright Star Mr. Bill Koikos greeted us in his kind and gentle manner and made sure we were seated in a good location. After we had finished a delicious meal of Greek snapper, he gave us a mint, asked if the food was good, and thanked us profusely for coming to the Bright Star. In about 1970, Mrs. Koikos began helping at the restaurant. I remember her bringing slices of her warm homemade bread to the table. She sat down beside us and began to chat, always asking about our family and making us feel like honored guests in her home. She made me feel so special. I thought it was because her daughter, Helen, and I were such good friends, but I soon learned she made everyone feel that special. Anastasia and Bill Koikos passed on that generous spirit to their children, Helen, Jimmy, and Nicky, and it is one of the reasons people still feel so at home at the Bright Star.

Much of our social life revolves around the Bright Star. High school reunions, class luncheons, family birthday celebrations, and lunch with family and friends are just a few examples. We celebrated Jim Ed's sixty-fifth birthday in 1995 at the Bright Star with about seventy people in attendance. Jimmy, Nicky, and B. J. [Salser] handled every detail.

Nearly every Friday night we have dinner at the Bright Star with Buddy and Paddy Moore and Eddie and Karel Dunlavy, and I love to try Chef Austin [Davis]'s recommendation for the evening. Kathy [Walden] handles our order impeccably, and she makes sure we have the most luscious salads. No matter when we come, Marlon [Tanksley] is always there to make sure we are taken care of. Jim Ed goes to the Saturday morning Breakfast Club for good food, games, and gossip with his buddies, some of whom finished high school with him in 1948. Ten to twelve friends enjoy lunch each Sunday after church with Sonya [Twitty] as our server. When the First Methodist Church has a newly appointed preacher, Eddie Dunlavy always has a talk with him, explaining that the service must end by 11:50 so we can get to the Bright Star before the other churches.

Even after Frances Thames retired from writing the social column for the Bessemer News, she sat at a front table at the Bright Star where she saw everyone who came in. She invited you over to her table, quizzed you about any party you had been to, what everyone was wearing, what the hostess served, who came in with whom, and where you were going next. She loved Bessemer, and even in retirement she kept up with the news.

Our three sons grew up on Bright Star fare. Our son who lives in New York City always makes a visit to the Bright Star when he's home. In fact, when he calls to say he's coming to town, I ask what he would like for me to cook for him. Invariably he answers, "What night are we going to the Bright Star?" Our two sons who live in Birmingham come as often as possible, usually bringing their families or friends to the "Star of their hometown."

When our grandchildren arrived, they followed the family tradition of enjoying good food at the Bright Star. Our first two grandchildren at ages five and six insisted they could each eat an order of Greek tenderloin of beef. Jim Ed said, "No, you need to split one." He thought they couldn't eat that much (expensive) meat. Unfortunately for him, they proved him wrong and ate every morsel. So they continued to eat Greek tenderloin each time they came, and that was very frequently. Now they are nineteen and twenty, a sophomore and junior in college. They still say that the Bright Star tenderloin of beef is the best anywhere, and they can't wait to come to Bessemer and have some.

Congratulations and thank you, Bright Star, for providing one hundred years of hospitality, good times, and delicious food.

Jane White Mulkin

Just a thought from my fortieth birthday: my mom and stepfather treated me to lunch at the Bright Star. My mother does not like to go to a fancy place, but I managed since it was my birthday. I think my mother and stepfather enjoyed themselves more than I did. My stepfather has passed since then, but it is a special memory to me.

Gail A. Hendrix

My parents, J. W. and Glennis Pike, were (my mom still is) longtime patrons. I'm forty-four and grew up eating at the Bright Star. Your family was also so special to my mother and father. After my father's injury on June 29, 2001, Anne [Mull] would call the house every day to check on him until he was able to return home from the hospital. That went on for about two months. You can't imagine how much that meant to our family.

We've celebrated so many holidays, birthdays, etc., with your family that I hate not to send something.

Glynell Pike Ferguson

Hey folks,

I have been a loyal Bright Star customer for over twenty-five years!!!

My favorite memory happened one evening when my wife and I were sitting across the aisle from [football star] Bobby Humphrey and his wife. Jimmy Koikos "drifted" by, visiting his customers as he is so prone to do, and he asked Bobby to let him see the Super Bowl ring Bobby won while playing for the Denver Broncos. Jimmy put it on, and lo and behold, it was a perfect fit! Jimmy proceeded to walk away all the while exclaiming what a "perfect" fit it was and thanking Bobby profusely for the ring in front of everyone.

It was a hoot as you can guess and Bobby didn't know quite how to respond, but knowing Jimmy's playful nature, he soon had his precious Super Bowl ring back on his own hand!

Thanks for all the memories and those luscious Greek tenderloins!!!!

Mark L. Slay

Two Surprises at One Very Special Place, and Countless Fond Memories

We have been faithful fans of the Bright Star for as long as I can remember. There are two occasions that stand out as a testament to the importance of the Bright Star in our lives, and they both center around my late husband, E. W. Harris. E. W. was never one who wanted to be in the spotlight. So every time we wanted to celebrate a milestone event, we had to be crafty, and we always needed the Bright Star's help.

A Surprise Fiftieth Anniversary

When E. W. was undergoing chemotherapy for cancer and lost all of his hair, he certainly wasn't in the party mood. Our family wanted to celebrate our fiftieth wedding anniversary, yet he didn't want a big to-do. So dear friends Renee and Fred Ross invited close friends Edna and Shelton Roy, Sheila and Ron Morgan, and Frances and Hoyt Bence for a surprise private dinner for us at the Bright Star in 1992. E. W. thought we were just meeting Fred and Renee for dinner, and when we walked in the door, the guests were sitting around a table topped with fifty yellow roses and singing "Happy Anniversary." He was happily overwhelmed and we all cherished celebrating our fiftieth anniversary that evening. After he returned to a healthy state, our family sent us on a seven-day Caribbean cruise. Another reason for us to dine at the Bright Star to celebrate.

A Surprise Seventy-Fifth Birthday

My daughter Peggy Harris Hollis and her family of Houston, Texas, hosted a surprise birthday party for E. W. at the Bright Star over Labor Day weekend 1997. We got E. W. to the party by saying it was for the birthday of our dear friend Jeannette Hall (also a former Bright Star regular). When E. W. and the family walked in to the party, everyone started singing "Happy Birthday" and he began singing along as well, as he thought he was singing to Jeannette. The one hundred people in the room had a good laugh when he realized it was his own party he was singing for.

A Special Place in Our Hearts

As you can see, over the years the Bright Star has not only been a backdrop for all of our important celebrations (we celebrated my eighty-second birthday there on July 30, 2006), but they have also been special friends. Jimmy and Nicky Koikos and their wonderful staff have gone the extra mile to hide birthday cakes, accept flowers, sneak in guests and more—all to ensure that the surprise element, the dinner, and dessert go off without a hitch. And the Bright Star is not only for special occasions, as every time our family comes to town, that's the only place my daughter Peggy and her husband, Wayne, grandson John and his wife, Marsha Hollis, and granddaughter Brooke and her husband, Blake Hortenstine, request to eat. We have spent countless Sundays after church sharing wonderful meals and visiting with friends among the beautiful historical murals and photographs and the wonderful football memorabilia (Roll Tide!). From our family to yours a very, very happy one-hundredth anniversary to the Bright Star!

Mary Merle Harris

This letter is being sent to you to express my sincere and deep appreciation for the kindness extended to me on my frequent visits to the restaurant. You have gone out of your way to ensure my relaxation and enjoyment.

I especially recall the special efforts given to me whenever I came to visit the Bright Star whether I was alone, with family, or with friends. I remember on several occasions that dinner was a gala affair with all the trimmings, including candlelight. Those visits have very special meanings to me. The special attention given to me at (my eatery) home away from home is a great testament to your humanity. I truly believe that because of the generous hearts and gentle touches, people have continued to come generations over.

It is also evident that the management and staff have a deep and abiding sense of family. Thank you for making me feel that I am a part of your family.

We wish you continued success on your one-hundredth anniversary and many years to come.

Patricia Hendon (Mrs. Edward) May

Interviews

I began coming to the Bright Star before I was born. My mother was pregnant with me when she was eating at the Bright Star. My mother says I was raised on Bright Star food. Our family runs a real estate business founded by my dad in the 1940s. Like the Bright Star, our business is family owned and operated.

I've been coming here regularly since 1948. There were three kids in our family, all born within thirty-five months of each other. After church on Sundays, we'd go to the Bright Star and "Mr. Bill" would always seat us in one of the private booths in the back. Since we were what you could call "active," he didn't want us disturbing other customers.

My favorite meal has changed roughly every decade. As a child it was the veal cutlet with cream sauce. Then I switched to the roast beef with au jus. It is still featured at the Bright Star today. Then my taste switched to the fried shrimp, and later to the tenderloin Greek style. Now I'm hooked on the large Greek salad, boiled shrimp, and seafood gumbo.

I have a son who has also been coming here since before he was born, as I was eating at the Bright Star when I was carrying him. I guess I've eaten at the Bright Star at least once a week for the past fifty-two years, except for when I was out of town. It was not unusual for me to have lunch and dinner several times during a week as there were board meetings and other luncheons held here. I almost feel like I have a private booth here. I even take credit for the management having Greek potatoes on the menu at the Bright

Star. I told them how much I love potatoes prepared that way, and they began featuring them on the menu regularly.

We've had numerous family celebrations here, everything from Dad's sixtieth birthday with a belly dancer to Father's Day and Mother's Day luncheons. When we have friends or real estate clients move into this area, we always give them a tour of the city and bring them to the Bright Star.

We've had fifty-seven years of memories here, and the amazing thing is not one of them is bad. The food is always wonderful and the people treat us like members of the family. It's a great feeling to visit a restaurant and have the people there really care about you and make you feel so welcome.

Pam Segars Morris

I was about fourteen years old when I began coming here with my parents. We've brought our grandchildren here many times, and our grandson noticed the star on the sign outside and thought it was a cowboy place. He would ask us to take him to the cowboy restaurant.

You have a wonderful family atmosphere here. There's a closeness to this family that people recognize.

Vicki Briley

We've been married for twenty-eight years, so that gives you an idea about how long we've been fans of the Bright Star. Vicki grew up in the Concord area, and I was raised in Homewood. The Bright Star is a unique place with a special atmosphere. All these years and the Bright Star has never disappointed us a single time. Once, while we were looking for a place to eat in San Francisco, we were asking ourselves, "Wonder where their Bright Star is?" We've always felt that if the Bright Star ever closed, it would be like turning out the lights in Bessemer.

It's a very relaxed atmosphere, whether you are in a suit or wearing casual clothes. I remember coming here once and seeing all these black Suburbans parked outside. John Ashcroft was eating here with all his security people. A meal at the Bright Star is like having dinner with a friend.

Jim Briley

We moved to Bessemer in 1955 and began coming to the Bright Star around 1956. I remember the seats at the bar and I remember Bill and Tasia Koikos. They were really lovely people.

My husband and I used to travel a lot, and I remember we had just arrived in Los Angeles on a flight from Hong Kong. The pilot was greeting us as we were getting off the plane and asked where we were from.

We told him that we were from a small town named Bessemer just outside Birmingham. He said, "Oh, that's the place that has the Bright Star Restaurant!" We also met some people in Chicago who knew of the Bright Star. It seems that people know the Bright Star everywhere we've been.

We've eaten at many fine restaurants around the world, but we've never had a better meal than those we've enjoyed at the Bright Star. I guess I'm partial to the trout almondine, the beef tips, crab claws, and your fresh vegetables. When my late husband, Charles, owned Dixie Nissan, we had a company dinner party here at the restaurant. Later, when the Bright Star remodeled and opened their Dixie Room, they named it after our business. Jimmy and Nicky have done an excellent job in running a wonderful business their family began.

Betty Campbell

We've been married twenty-five years and began coming to the Bright Star before the children were born. When we'd come here, Jim would drive around the block with the kids. I'd go in and order our meal. Afterward, we always left an extra tip for the servers as they did such a great job getting us in and out so we wouldn't disturb other customers.

Our out-of-town guests also loved coming here. We'd all order different entrees so we could sample all the dishes.

Edwina Cameron

I was working at the Birmingham Southern Railroad about forty years ago before we were married. I would come to the Bright Star often to eat. We always had great meals at the Bright Star. We loved their fish and the fresh vegetables. Lunches and dinner at the Bright Star were always special occasions.

The Bright Star is also the perfect place for a business luncheon. We ate here often during recesses from cases being tried in the courthouse.

Jim Cameron

I began coming to the Bright Star in 1958 when I was eleven years old. We moved back to Bessemer from California, and I graduated from Bessemer High School in 1965. Mr. Bill was still here in those days. He always did a great job directing people in the reception area. It was a special event to eat here. I usually ordered the shrimp or other seafood. Then I loved the Greek snapper. After I graduated from the University of Alabama, I worked at Alabama Power before I was drafted into the army. I came back to Bessemer and worked at Alabama Power until I retired in 2001. Then I volunteered at the Bessemer Area Chamber of Commerce and became president of the organization. We promote economic development in the city and the members of the chamber.

We've seen a lot of activity in the Bessemer area recently. There are a lot of new businesses locating in western Jefferson County, especially along Highway 150, Morgan Road, and other areas. There is also a master plan for the redevelopment of the downtown district. The Realty Building has a number of tenants, and other buildings are featuring businesses on the street level with offices on the upper floors. We're promoting that type of development here. I call the Bright Star the "crown jewel" of our downtown area.

My special memories of the Bright Star include seeing Bear Bryant and Shug Jordan in here. Always brought my mother here on Mother's Day, too.

Part of going to the Bright Star years ago before the remodeling was waiting in line to get in. There was always a crowd. The restaurant shares a parking lot with the chamber, and I would often walk to lunch here. I remember noticing the license tags of cars from all over Alabama who came here to eat. Bessemer has always been close to my heart, and the Bright Star is the heart of Bessemer.

Ronnie Acker
President of the Bessemer Area Chamber of Commerce

I remember my first meal here. I ordered beef tips, and thought they were great. We were hooked, and have been coming back ever since.

All our family occasions are celebrated here. We have two sons and two daughters all within about thirty miles of each other.

Becky Middlebrooks

We've been coming here for about thirty years. Becky is from Tennessee and I'm from Marion, Alabama. We moved to Bessemer in 1975.

Our favorites must be the Greek snapper, the flounder, and the beef tenderloin. We've gotten to know all the servers, and enjoy each of them. Jimmy always seats us in our favorite place.

I remember seeing Gene Stallings, Bear Bryant, Senator Shelby, and other celebrities here. And I remember Bill and Tasia. They were always here and always spoke to us. The Bright Star is a true family restaurant.

Jim Middlebrooks

My earliest memories of the Bright Star were of the crowds that were always here. My dad worked at Woodward Iron back in the 1920s. Bessemer was really an active place back then. Several trains ran through town each day, many of them carrying the miners who were getting off work on Friday afternoons. Some of those trains were so full there was no place to sit. Men were just hanging on the side rails like in the cable cars of San Francisco.

Many of those guys were eager to visit the "houses of interest" that a number of "madams" operated here in town. Some of the miners went straight there before going anyplace else. They were often still covered in coal dust. It was often said that some of those "ladies of interest" would have blond hair on Friday afternoons, but their hair was coal black on Monday mornings.

Downtown Bessemer was pretty lively in those days. There was an A & P grocery store, Kress, Woolworth's, and others. And Bessemer High School became a premium school. A lot was expected of students there. In the 1950s, the city shifted from a manufacturing to a service economy, and the character of the city changed.

For about fifty years, I always thought of the Bright Star as Bessemer's upscale restaurant. There were several other pretty good restaurants in town, but there was only one Bright Star. Maybe it was because of its Greek influence. I remember Bill always being dressed in a suit. He always had a quiet dignity about him. We have operated White's True Value Hardware Store down the street for about forty years, and Miss Tasia would always bring us coffee in the mornings. I treasure those memories to this day. I remember Gus Sarris as well. He was always cheerful, and was very positive in his dealings with other people. I didn't know Pete that well. All the waiters were top notch, and when the women began working as servers, they were also the best.

Mitch Abercrombie

I'm from Mobile and I love seafood. My wife is from this area and she first told me about the Bright Star. We started coming here regularly and got to know the people here. We've seen people from all walks of life here. Once, I met [Senator Russ Feingold], who was dining here. He told me that Senator Howell Heflin was always talking about the Bright Star. Since he was visiting in the area, he decided he had to come here to eat.

Over the years, we've developed a special relationship with the family and the staff here. I remember once when our wedding anniversary came around, my wife, Patricia, and I were going to eat at the Bright Star. I called Jimmy and asked him to set something up for us for dinner. When we arrived, the staff noticed that I did not have any flowers. One of the servers asked me if I had brought flowers and I admit-

ted that I remembered the anniversary but did not think to bring flowers for my wife. While we were eating, they went to a florist, got some flowers and a card, and brought them back for me to give to my wife. To this day, I've never forgotten how thoughtful they were. I can't say it saved my marriage, but I can say that it saved me that night!

As the mayor, I love what the Bright Star has done for our city. As a customer, I love the food and the people here. The longevity of the staff here speaks volumes for the management of the restaurant.

The Bright Star is truly a bright spot in the City of Bessemer. I only wish it was bigger to accommodate more people!

Edward E. May
Mayor of Bessemer

I have been coming to the Bright Star for more than twenty years now. Friday nights here are very special to us. We love the personal attention we get from the servers, especially Kathy [Walden]. We love the exceptional food and visiting with the many people we know here.

Buddy Moore

I had a grocery store in town for years. I began coming to the Bright Star fifty years ago, and I usually visited about three or four times a week.

We love the great food and the wonderful, friendly service. Kathy [Walden] is usually our server and she does a great job. The Bright Star has a real personal touch, not like the corporate restaurants.

Frank D'Allesandro

We've been eating here for forty-one years. I think we're here almost every Friday night. And we love celebrating special events such as birthdays at the Bright Star.

We love the servers, Kathy [Walden] especially. They all make you feel so welcome here. Jimmy does a great job as a host.

Mrs. Paul Franklin

The Bright Star is unique because of the memorable meals. The food here is outstanding. I always order the fresh fish. Jimmy is so careful about overseeing the restaurant. The service is unusually good.

Paul Franklin

I've had many great meals here. I used to model for the Pizitz and Loveman's department stores and ate here many times. I remember one time when I finished my meal I found I had left my money in another purse at home. I asked to talk to Nicky and he told me not to worry. He told me I could pay the next time I was here.

I live in Tampa, Florida, now and come to the Bright Star when I'm in town visiting relatives. As a matter of fact, I'm leaving right now to return to Tampa, and I have a pie to go that I'm taking with me! How about that, a whole pineapple-cheese pie that's going all the way to Florida!

Melinda Miles

We have been coming to the Bright Star for many years. We lived in Cahaba Heights and drove here. The food is consistently great, the prices are reasonable, and the service is exceptional.

We had our parents' fiftieth-anniversary party here and my uncle's sixtieth anniversary. If there was a special event in our family, we always wanted to celebrate at the Bright Star.

Gene Fievet

We've been coming here for about twenty-five years—it's a way of life for us. My late wife and I would eat lunch here almost every Sunday. I'd sometimes say we'd call if we weren't coming.

The Bright Star is different from other restaurants because the food is consistently good. Some places are good sometimes and not so good at others. We are assured of getting a great meal each time we visit the Bright Star. We love the menu items and we love the servers. Jeff [Golson] is usually the one who waits on us.

Norman Ponder

We've been coming here for a very long time and we've never had a bad experience. We love Neda [Arthur]. She is so adorable and makes us feel so welcome—always says she's "cooking with gas!" And we remember Cliff [Isom]. He always greeted us and made us feel that we had come to the right place.

Coming to the Bright Star was like visiting someone in their home. I particularly loved the lamb, the turkey, and the fresh vegetables. And we loved the family atmosphere here. Once when I walked in late for a reservation, I told Jimmy, "We're late," and he replied, "You're never late."

Grace Reid

I started eating here when I was about ten years old. I am ninety now. The Bright Star is different from other restaurants because it is a real family place. I remember Mr. Bill and Miss Tasia. They were lovely people and they were good friends with my mom and dad.

I especially like the Greek potatoes. I like to say that I'm the reason they have them on the menu. I used to tell them that I loved those Greek potatoes.

Norman Jones

I loved [Bill and Tasia Koikos]. They were lovely people. I remember eating here on Saturdays with my father, and it was such a delight. We came to see Mr. Bill and Mr. Pete. Tasia brought homemade bread to our table and treated us like family. I remember "Post Office" John Bonduris who ran the pool hall in the basement for years. Going to the Bright Star was always a special event for us.

Cameron Grammas

We've been enjoying Sunday lunch here since 1969. We love to sit in the 1907 Room and remember Anne Mull and Liz Gardner.

The food is always good. I especially love the trout and the country fried steak and fresh vegetables. The Bright Star has the best coffee around.

Donald and Joyce Smith

I'm from Virginia and have been in Birmingham for about twenty years, but this is my first visit to the Bright Star. My girlfriend, Kelly, and I were driving around and decided to come here to see if everything we've heard about the restaurant is true.

We saw the big crowd here and knew it must be a good place to eat. And the atmosphere is great. The Bright Star really represents the best of Bessemer.

Mark Roberts

I've been eating here for about thirty years. I remember walking by the restaurant when I was going to a movie at the Grand Theatre in town.

I always look forward to a meal at the Bright Star. We had our daughter's wedding party here. It is a very special place.

Litton Battle

It seems like we've been eating here for a hundred years. We love the food and the reception we get when we come here. Jimmy and Nicky greet us the same way their mother and father did years ago. The family atmosphere has not changed.

Our love for the Koikos family has made it a special place for us. We've been married for fifty-six years, and Mrs. Koikos was at our home for our wedding. It was a hot day in August so long ago. We lived on Dartmouth Avenue, too.

We always see friends of ours here. And the food is consistently good. I remember the very first shrimp I ever ate was at the Bright Star.

I hope this place will be here for another hundred years!

Jack and Sue Pearson

I grew up in this area, and dinner at the Bright Star was a real event. The people here made it so special. I can't think of one special event celebrated here because each visit to the Bright Star was a special event.

We've been coming here three or four times a week for the last ten years. Miss Neda [Arthur] knows me so well by now that she can tell me what I'll enjoy that day before I even look at the menu. These little things set the restaurant apart.

Cliff [Isom] always parked our car and was so friendly. When you were talking to Cliff, you were a very important person to him. He loved what he did.

Carol Noe

My favorite dish here is the Greek tenderloin. It's always good. I'd come here for breakfast if they still served it. My entire family enjoys coming here. I brought my son-in-law, who lives in San Francisco, here and he loves it, too. When my son gets a new girlfriend, he brings her to the Bright Star to impress her.

I started coming here in 1950 as a nine-year-old boy with my dad, who delivered bread here for Home Baking Company. I'd ride with him on Saturday mornings. We'd come here and Dad would drink coffee with the SAPS group and I'd have a Coke. The most frightening things to me were the big coffee urns. They were big, shiny things in the back. For a nine-year-old, they were pretty impressive. Mr. Bill and Mr. Pete would climb up a ladder to clean them.

Mr. Bill always called me Mr. Simmons. I asked him not to do that, but he told me that it's the way things are supposed to be. Dad's lodge used to have banquets here. He later became a minister. It was a real treat to come here for Sunday lunch.

Mr. Bill was a real pleasure to be around. Miss Tasia used to bake bread and bring us some. My dad sometimes brought her the flour from Home Baking Company that she used to bake her bread. Also for the piecrust for some of the restaurant's pies. I remember Jimmy, Nicky, and Helen working here. Helen was working as a cashier.

As for servers, Anne [Mull] was probably the most entertaining. She always had a joke. Margaret [Dunkin] was an old friend. B. J. [Salser] and I have been friends for a long time too.

I've eaten at restaurants in London, Barcelona, Nice, Monte Carlo, Rome, Malaga, Turkey, Athens, Venice, and other places. They all had good food, but I was always glad to get back to the Bright Star. Once, I brought one of [the Bright Star's] pies with me to Pennsylvania. I had it on the plane and the stewardesses wanted me to share with them. I gave each of them a small piece.

My dad, Mr. Bill, and Mr. Pete were all good friends. When Mr. Bill died, I told Jimmy that we had lost one of the finest gentlemen in this town. When my dad died, Jimmy came to me and told me that we just lost one of the last true gentlemen in Bessemer.

Miss Tasia was a lovely lady. She loved Mr. Bill and she loved this business. Jimmy and Nicky are both married to this place now. It's their family.

Will Simmons

I was born in 1916 and have been coming here since the 1920s. A friend of mine was working here in the kitchen. Gus Sarris was here in those days. Dude Ammons, my dad, came here from Phenix City about the time the Cain brothers, Bob, Paul, Sam, and Jim, did. They had a barbershop in town.

I've enjoyed all the meals I've had at the Bright Star.

Mr. Ammons

I lived here from 1940 until 1949, but I could not afford to eat here until I came back fifty years later.

I think it is wonderful to be one hundred years old and still provide the food, service, and atmosphere that you can't find in a lot of places.

My wife, Betty, and I had our fiftieth wedding anniversary here. It was a great night—one of those nights you always want to remember for the food and service and the restaurant that provided it. It is something you treasure today, because you don't find landmarks like this anymore. It is so hard to survive today in the restaurant industry as an independent. The Bright Star means a lot to Bessemer, and Bessemer means a lot to the Bright Star.

Jimmy knows his business. I have traveled all over the world and eaten at restaurants in the United States, Europe, the Far East, and South America and the one thing that stands out about a good restau-

rant is the maitre d'. Jimmy is a maitre d'—he stands there and knows and controls this restaurant. This restaurant is Jimmy and Nicky's, and the atmosphere of the restaurant reflects their personalities.

We just recently celebrated our fifty-fourth wedding anniversary—just Betty and me. Jimmy had Chef Austin come out and ask us what we wanted, and he prepared a special, personal anniversary dinner for us. It was one of the finest dinners you could ever have had. Again, I have eaten in the best restaurants in the world, and the food is equal to anything I have ever had in my travels.

Lew Shealy

For the last fifteen years we have been part of a Friday night group. A lot of the same people come on Friday night, so we see all our friends here. We have a very special person here, Nancy [Whittington], who takes care of all our needs. She babies our husbands and she is so nice to us. That is a big reason we eat here. A big reason, also, that we eat here is that the food is consistently great. We love the friendships and the company.

Gayle Hagar

We have come to the Bright Star with various friends over the years. We started out thirty years ago with a dozen. Now there are five to seven. We remember [Tasia], how she oversaw things and how hard she worked. She was very hospitable.

We always feel welcome here. When we call for reservations, they know us. They make us feel special. I have had clients I brought here. They never fail to ask to come back.

Howard Garrett

We have been eating here for thirty years. I remember seeing Mrs. Koikos walking up and down the aisle.

We currently come two or three times a week. If we did not live in Vestavia, we would eat here every day. Food and service make this a special place. All of the servers are the kindest and friendliest people. We have gotten to know them personally, send birthday cards, etc.

I love the red snapper and peanut butter pie, and our little granddaughters like to come to the Bright Star. If I were going for an MBA in the food business, I would forget school and just get a job here and follow Jimmy around. I admire so many of your people here, like Marlon. He is so capable and works so hard.

We have enjoyed watching the restaurant grow. It is great to observe a business grow, based on the food and service provided.

Stanley and Shirley Paradise

I would come on Friday night. When we wanted to bring out-of-town guests somewhere unique, we would bring them here. Invariably, they would talk about it for years to come. People that eat out a lot want to eat here for sure.

Barbara Lee

Today is my ninetieth birthday. I have been coming here regularly for twenty-two years following the death of my husband. I am usually by myself. I eat here because it is the best place in Birmingham area.

Leslie Sibley Powell

Longtime Bright Star server Anne Mull with Nicky and Jimmy Koikos. (Courtesy of the Lucas Family.)

Tom D. Bonduris, founder of the Bright Star and owner from 1907 until 1924. (Courtesy of the Koikos family.)

Peter D. Koikos, co-owner of the Bright Star from 1924 until 1960. (Courtesy of the Koikos family.)

John D. Bonduris, co-owner of the Bright Star from 1924 until 1944. (Courtesy of the Koikos family.)

Gus E. Sarris, co-owner of the Bright Star from 1924 until 1969. (Courtesy of the Koikos family.)

Bill D. Koikos, co-owner of the Bright Star from 1924 until 1974. (Courtesy of the Koikos family.)

Left to right: Tom P. Bonduris, Gus E. Sarris, and John D. Bonduris holding son John D. Bonduris, Jr., ca. 1928. (Courtesy of the Bonduris family.)

Koikos family portrait, 1946. Front row, left to right: Helen, Bill, Nicky, Anastasia, and Jimmy Koikos. Back row: Nicholas Microyiannakis, father of Anastasia Koikos. (Courtesy of the Koikos family.)

Helen and Bill Koikos in Athens, Greece, August 1952. (Courtesy of the Koikos family.)

Left to right: Bill Koikos, Frances Raymond, unknown server, Irene Higgs, Jimmy Koikos, and Thelma Herring at the Bright Star, 1958. (Courtesy of the Koikos family.)

Peter D. Koikos and his wife, Thalia, ca. 1965. (Courtesy of the Koikos family.)

Nicky, Bill, and Jimmy Koikos behind the cash register at the Bright Star, ca. 1970.
(Courtesy of the Koikos family.)

Bill Koikos's ninety-second birthday celebration at his home in December 1986. Seated: Bill Koikos. Standing, left to right: Nicky, Tasia, and Jimmy Koikos, Stacey, Connie, Joanna, and Helen Cocoris. (Courtesy of the Koikos family.)

Nicky and Jimmy Koikos at the Bright Star, 2006. (Courtesy of Bob Farley.)

Koikos home in Peleta, ca. 1950. (Courtesy of the Koikos family.)

Helen Koikos, Eleni Koikos (seated), and Anastasia Koikos in Peleta, Greece, 1962. This was the first time Anastasia had met her mother-in-law, who was 104 years old. (Courtesy of the Koikos family.)

Pete Koikos, Gus Sarris, and Bill Koikos at a retirement party for Gus Sarris, 1969. (Courtesy of the Koikos family.)

Nicky and Jimmy Koikos, standing, with Junius Harris and Bill Koikos in the 1907 Room, 1984. (Courtesy of the Koikos family.)

Jimmy Koikos visiting Coach Paul "Bear" Bryant on the Crimson Tide practice field in Tuscaloosa, 1979. (Courtesy of the Koikos family.)

Jimmy and Nicky Koikos during construction of the 1907 Room, 1978. (Courtesy of the Cocoris family.)

Alabama head coach Ray Perkins with Bright Star manager Nick Costas at the Bright Star. Family friend Jackie Marino stands at the far left. (Courtesy of the Koikos family.)

Members of the Bonduris family visit the Bright Star, 1984. Seated, left to right: Jimmy Koikos, Bill Koikos, and Sammy Bonduris. Standing, left to right: John D. Bonduris, Jr. (Sammy's brother), and Nicky Koikos. (Courtesy of the Koikos family.)

Above:
Bill Koikos with his three granddaughters, 1984. From left, Joanna, Connie, and Stacey Cocoris. (Courtesy of the Cocoris family.)

Tasia and Bill Koikos celebrating their fiftieth wedding anniversary, 1986. (Courtesy of the Cocoris family.)

Alabama head football coach Mike Shula, far right; Nicky Koikos, far left; and Bright Star employees (left to right) Austin Davis, Tony Feagins, Marcus Patrick, and Carl Thomas. (Courtesy of the Koikos family.)

Alabama head football coach Gene Stallings at the Bright Star with Jimmy Koikos, 1997. (Courtesy of the Koikos family.)

The Bright Star's breakfast club, August 5, 2006. Front row, left to right: Frank D'Alessandro, Jim Ed Mulkin, Jimmy Koikos, and Lee Roberts. Middle row, left to right: Jim Cain, Jim Byram, John Vines, Jimmy Creel, Mitch Abercrombie, Lew Shealy, Hugh Hudson, and Eddie Dunlavy. Top row: Andy LaRussa. (Courtesy of the Koikos family.)

Wedding reception at thc Bright Star, 2005. (Courtesy of the Koikos family.)

(Courtesy of Bob Farley.)